The Gospel According to Mark

Part One

The Gospel According to Mark

Part One

Mark 1:1–9:32

Marie Noonan Sabin
with Little Rock Scripture Study staff

Little Rock Scripture Study

LITURGICAL PRESS
Collegeville, Minnesota

www.littlerockscripture.org

Nihil obstat for the commentary text by Marie Noonan Sabin: Robert C. Harren, *Censor deputatus.*
Imprimatur for the commentary text by Marie Noonan Sabin: ✠ John F. Kinney, Bishop of St. Cloud, Minnesota, December 2, 2005.

Cover design by John Vineyard. Interior art by Ned Bustard. Map on page 10 created by Ann Blattner. Map on page 78 created by Clifford M. Yeary with Ann Blattner.

This symbol indicates material that was created by Little Rock Scripture Study to supplement the biblical text and commentary. Some of these inserts first appeared in the *Little Rock Catholic Study Bible*; others were created specifically for this book by Catherine Upchurch and Michael DiMassa.

Library of Congress Cataloging-in-Publication Data

Names: Sabin, Marie Noonan, author. | Little Rock Scripture Study Staff, author.
Title: The gospel according to Mark / Marie Noonan Sabin with Little Rock Scripture Study staff.
Description: Collegeville : Liturgical Press, 2020. | Includes commentary from author's previously published work and excerpts adapted from Little Rock Catholic Study Bible. | Contents: Part one: Mark 1-9:32 — Part two: Mark 9:33-16. | Summary: "A Bible study of the Gospel According to Mark. Part One covers Mark 1:1-9:32, providing an in-depth study of Jesus' ministry of healing and preaching. Part Two explores Mark 9:33-16:20, including Jesus' entry into Jerusalem and the events of his passion, death, and resurrection. Commentary, study and reflection questions, prayers, and access to online lectures are included for each volume"— Provided by publisher.
Identifiers: LCCN 2020000472 (print) | LCCN 2020000473 (ebook) | ISBN 9780814665190 (paperback) | ISBN 9780814665442 (paperback) | ISBN 9780814665206 (v. 1 ; epub) | ISBN 9780814665206 (v. 1 ; mobi) | ISBN 9780814665206 (v. 1 ; pdf) | ISBN 9780814665459 (v. 2 ; epub) | ISBN 9780814665459 (v. 2 ; mobi) | ISBN 9780814665459 (v. 2 ; pdf)
Subjects: LCSH: Bible. Mark—Textbooks.
Classification: LCC BS2586 .S23 2020 (print) | LCC BS2586 (ebook) | DDC 226.3/077—dc22
LC record available at https://lccn.loc.gov/2020000472
LC ebook record available at https://lccn.loc.gov/2020000473

TABLE OF CONTENTS

Wrap-Up Lectures and Discussion Tips for Facilitators are available for each lesson at no charge. Find them online at LittleRockScripture.org/Lectures/MarkPartOne.

Welcome

The Bible is at the heart of what it means to be a Christian. It is the Spirit-inspired word of God for us. It reveals to us the God who created, redeemed, and guides us still. It speaks to us personally and as a church. It forms the basis of our public liturgical life and our private prayer lives. It urges us to live worthily and justly, to love tenderly and wholeheartedly, and to be a part of building God's kingdom here on earth.

Though it was written a long time ago, in the context of a very different culture, the Bible is no relic of the past. Catholic biblical scholarship is among the best in the world, and in our time and place, we have unprecedented access to it. By making use of solid scholarship, we can discover much about the ancient culture and religious practices that shaped those who wrote the various books of the Bible. With these insights, and by praying with the words of Scripture, we allow the words and images to shape us as disciples. By sharing our journey of faithful listening to God's word with others, we have the opportunity to be stretched in our understanding and to form communities of love and learning. Ultimately, studying and praying with God's word deepens our relationship with Christ.

The Gospel According to Mark, Part One
Mark 1:1–9:32

The resource you hold in your hands is divided into five lessons. Each lesson involves personal prayer and study using this book *and* the experience of group prayer, discussion, and wrap-up lecture.

If you are using this resource in the context of a small group, we suggest that you meet five times, discussing one lesson per meeting. Allow about 90 minutes for the small group gathering. Small groups function best with eight to twelve people to ensure good group dynamics and to allow all to participate as they wish.

Some groups choose to have an initial gathering before their regular sessions begin. This allows an opportunity to meet one another, pass out books, and, if desired, view the optional intro lecture for this study available on the "Resources" page of the Little Rock Scripture Study website (www.littlerockscripture.org). Please note that there is only one intro lecture for two-part studies.

Every Bible study group is a little bit different. Some of our groups like to break each lesson up into two weeks of study so they are reading less each week and have more time to discuss the questions together at their weekly gatherings. If your group wishes to do this, simply agree how much of each lesson will be read each week, and only answer the questions that correspond to the material you read. Wrap-up lectures can then be viewed at the end of every other meeting rather than at the end of every meeting. Of course, this will mean that your study will last longer, and your group will meet more times.

WHAT MATERIALS WILL YOU USE?

The materials in this book include:

- The text of the Gospel of Mark, chapters 1:1–9:32, using the New American Bible, Revised Edition as the translation.
- Commentary by Marie Noonan Sabin (which has also been published separately as part of the New Collegeville Bible Commentary series).
- Occasional inserts highlighting elements of the chapters of Mark being studied. Some of these appear also in the *Little Rock Catholic Study Bible* while others are supplied by staff writers.
- Questions for study, reflection, and discussion at the end of each lesson.
- Opening and closing prayers for each lesson, as well as other prayer forms available in the closing pages of the book.

In addition, there are wrap-up lectures available for each lesson. Your group may choose to purchase a DVD containing these lectures or make use of the audio or video lectures online at no charge. The link to these free lectures is: LittleRockScripture.org/Lectures/MarkPartOne. Of course, if your group has access to qualified speakers, you may choose to have live presentations.

Each person will need a current translation of the Bible. We recommend the *Little Rock Catholic Study Bible*, which makes use of the New American Bible, Revised Edition. Other translations, such as the New Jerusalem Bible or the New Revised Standard Version: Catholic Edition, would also work well.

HOW WILL YOU USE THESE MATERIALS?

Prepare in advance

Using Lesson One as an example:

- Begin with a simple prayer like the one found on page 11.

- Read the assigned material in the printed book for Lesson One (pages 12–22) so that you are prepared for the weekly small group session. You may do this assignment by reading a portion over a period of several days (effective and manageable) or by preparing all at once (more challenging).
- Answer the questions, Exploring Lesson One, found at the end of the assigned reading, pages 23–25.
- Use the Closing Prayer on page 25 when you complete your study. This prayer may be used again when you meet with the group.

Meet with your small group

- After introductions and greetings, allow time for prayer (about 5 minutes) as you begin the group session. You may use the prayer found on page 11 (also used by individuals in their preparation) or use a prayer of your choosing.
- Spend about 45–50 minutes discussing the responses to the questions that were prepared in advance. You may also develop your discussion further by responding to questions and interests that arise during the discussion and faith-sharing itself.
- Close the discussion and faith-sharing with prayer, about 5–10 minutes. You may use the Closing Prayer at the end of each lesson or one of your choosing at the end of the book. It is important to allow people to pray for personal and community needs and to give thanks for how God is moving in your lives.
- Listen to or view the wrap-up lecture associated with each lesson (15–20 minutes). You may watch the lecture online, use a DVD, or provide a live lecture by a qualified local speaker. This lecture provides a common focus for the group and reinforces insights from each lesson. You may view the lecture together at the end of the session or, if your group runs out of time, you may invite group members to watch the lecture on their own time after the discussion.

Above all, be aware that the Holy Spirit is moving within and among you.

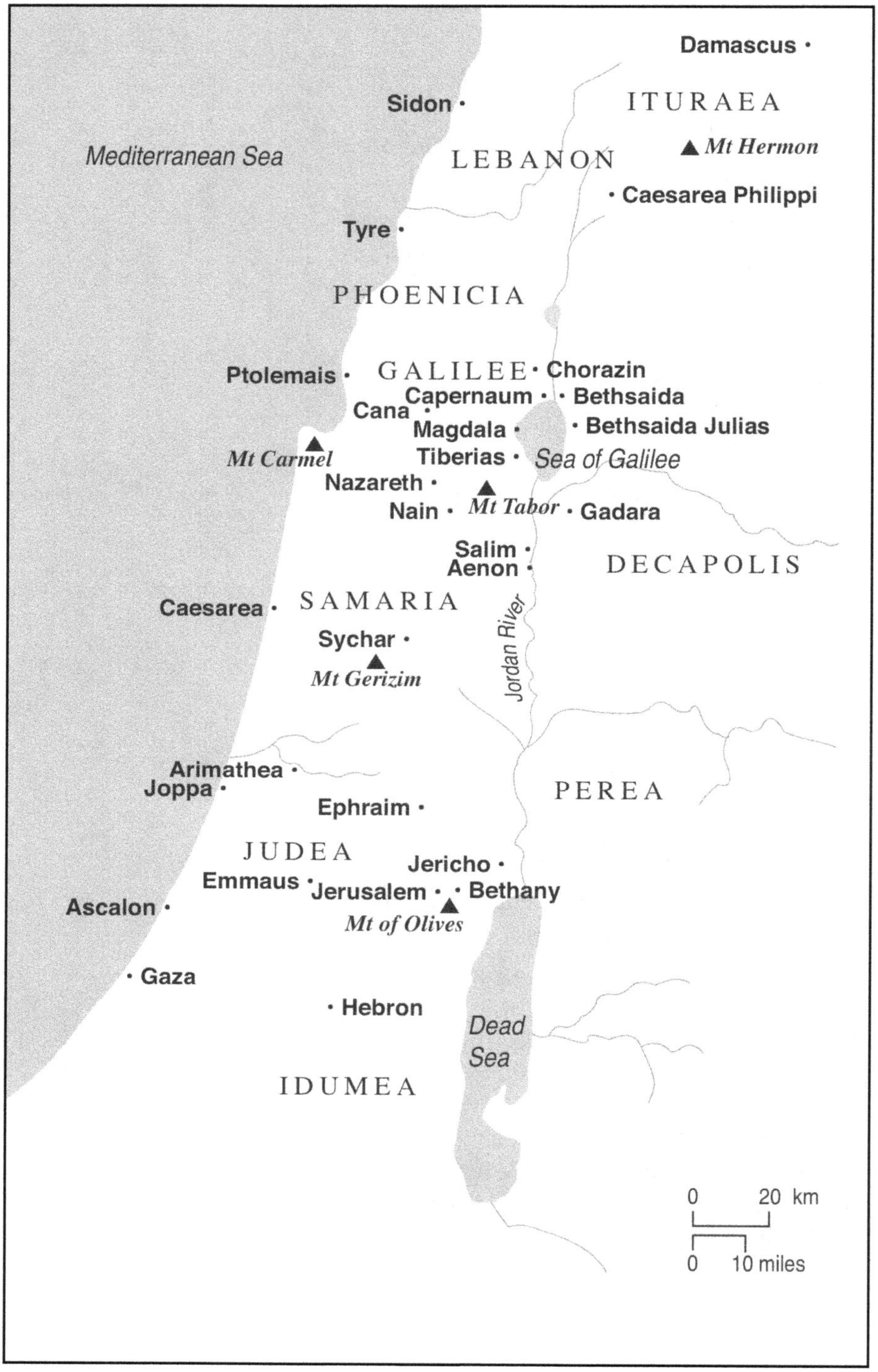

Palestine in the Time of Jesus

The Gospel According to Mark

Part One

LESSON ONE

Introduction and Mark 1

Begin your personal study and group discussion with a simple and sincere prayer such as:

Prayer

Loving God, open my mind and heart to hear your voice. Increase my understanding and inspire in me a greater desire to follow Jesus.

Read the Introduction on pages 12–15 and the Bible text of Mark 1 found in the outside columns of pages 17–22, highlighting what stands out to you.

Read the accompanying commentary to add to your understanding.

Respond to the questions on pages 23–25, Exploring Lesson One.

The Closing Prayer on page 25 is for your personal use and may be used at the end of group discussion.

INTRODUCTION

Author

The actual author of the Gospel of Mark, like those of all the Gospels, is unknown to us. The manuscripts that survived date from the fourth century; the names of the evangelists were added sometime in the second century. There is reason to believe that the early church was less interested in knowing the actual authorship than in connecting the Gospel narratives with apostolic witnesses. They found the names "Matthew" and "John" within their respective Gospels, and the name "Luke" as one mentioned by Paul as his traveling companion. For Mark they relied on a fragment written by a second-century bishop named Papias, who spoke of Mark as the "interpreter" of Peter. This suggestion dovetailed with the observation in Acts that Peter had visited the home of someone in Jerusalem named "John who is called Mark" (Acts 12:12). Some also found support in the reference in the first letter of Peter to "Mark, my son" (1 Pet 5:13). Not all scholars accept these inferences, yet the link with Peter is supported by internal evidence.

Audience

Since we do not know for certain who wrote the Gospel of Mark, we also cannot be certain of its intended audience. The link with Peter has led some scholars to speculate that it was addressed, like Peter's first letter, to the church in Rome. But there are many other bases for speculating both about Mark's Gospel and Peter's letter. Among them is the fact that Peter is known in Acts as the head of the Jerusalem church; an argument could be made that Mark was a member of that early Jewish-Christian community.

Language

Language offers some internal clues as to both the author and his intended audience. Mark's manuscript, like the other Gospels, has come down to us as a Greek text. Why, one might wonder, would the evangelists have written in Greek instead of in Hebrew or Aramaic, the Semitic idiom common in Galilee? The most probable reason is that from the time that Alexander of Greece conquered the Mesopotamian world, three centuries before the time of Jesus, Greek was the language of educated people. In fact, in the time of Alexander, the Jews translated their Bible into Greek (the "Septuagint"). Educated Jews knew the Bible in Greek as well as in Hebrew and Aramaic. There is good evidence that when the evangelists quote or refer to the Jewish Bible, they are following the Septuagint.

Mark's Gospel is not written in fluent Greek, however. The overall impression it leaves is that of an author who thought in one language and was trying to write in another.

Date and historical setting

The date of Mark's Gospel is also a matter of speculation. Most, although not all, scholars believe that Mark's was the earliest of the Gospels, written around 70 C.E. and followed in the eighties by Matthew and Luke, and in the nineties by John.

The year 70 was significant for all Jews, including the Jewish followers of Jesus, because it was the year that the Romans destroyed the Temple in Jerusalem. The destruction was the traumatic end to the four-year revolt of the Jews against Rome. The Temple had been destroyed once before by Babylon, six centuries earlier, and the effect had been devastating. The Roman destruction was also a watershed in Jewish history.

This time the Temple was never rebuilt. The leaders of the revolt (the Zealots), along with the Temple leaders (priests and Sadducees), disappeared or scattered. Judaism itself might have disappeared had it not been for the Pharisees. The Pharisees' reputation in the New Testament as rigid legalists is ill-deserved. They were, in fact, a devout lay group who had developed a flexible and creative approach to the interpretation of Scripture and had also fostered ways of bringing the prayers of the Temple into Jewish homes. When the Temple was lost, they provided the foundations for a continuing and vital Judaism. As the ancestors of modern rabbinic Judaism, they deserve the respect of modern Christians.

Why, then, are the Pharisees vilified in the New Testament? The answer does not lie in the time of Jesus. Indeed, many of the teachings of Jesus are so close to those of the Pharisees that some scholars have proposed that he is shown arguing with them because he was a member of their school. Judaism before the fall of the Temple was tolerant of many different forms of expression, and historical studies suggest that Christianity did not begin as a consciously separate religion, but as a new formulation of the ancient Jewish faith. After the Temple fell, however, Judaism regrouped, and the Pharisaic leaders became less tolerant of diversity within their ranks. In that new atmosphere, Jewish followers of Jesus were regarded with suspicion and put out of the synagogues. The Christian-Jewish community responded with anger. In the context of the post-seventies, the Pharisees appeared hostile to Jesus, and it is that hostility (and their own anger) that the evangelists retroactively projected into their accounts of Jesus' time.

Modern Judaism and modern Christianity may have developed along clearly different paths, but readers of the Gospels need to understand that Jesus and his disciples, as well as the evangelists Mark, Matthew, and John (Luke was Gentile), saw themselves as faithful Jews. Matthew's diatribes against "the scribes and the Pharisees" and John's scornful use of "the Jews" must be understood in the context of their own times, not that of Jesus.

The way each Gospel expresses its attitude toward Jews and Judaism is one criterion for dating it. John's denunciation of "the Jews" is one reason for placing his Gospel at the end of the century. Luke's way of distancing Christianity from Judaism (especially in Acts) suggests that he is not writing in its earliest moments. The Gospels of Mark and Matthew, on the other hand, are clearly composed in the context of a deep regard for Judaism itself. So, while all the Gospels are steeped in the Jewish Scriptures, Mark and Matthew especially present Jesus in the light of them.

The relevance of the "Old Testament" to the New Testament

Christians reading the New Testament today will miss much of its meaning and most of its richness if they are unfamiliar with the references to the "Old" or First Testament that form its framework and substructure. This commentary, therefore, tries to present the reader with all the scriptural quotes, allusions, and echoes that provide the basis of Mark's theological thought.

The most significant biblical background in this Gospel comes from the Wisdom writings. In Catholic tradition, there are seven Jewish Wisdom writings: Proverbs, Psalms, Job, Ecclesiastes, the Song of Songs, Sirach, and the Wisdom of Solomon. Each of these works is distinct, yet they share certain significant things in common. They are all set in domestic situations and everyday life. Many of them use a pithy style of speech. They are all focused on how to live a wise and holy life. They all agree that "fear of the LORD [in the sense of holy awe] is the beginning of wisdom" (Prov 9:10). Most important, three of them (Proverbs, Sirach, and the Wisdom of Solomon) imagine God's Wisdom as a personified attribute that walks on earth and dwells among human beings. God's Wisdom was there from the beginning and created the world and all that is in it. God's Wisdom is imagined as a maternal figure—life-giving, nurturing and healing, restorative and transfiguring. When Mark wanted to communicate the significance of Jesus, it was quite natural for him to present him as God's Wisdom made flesh.

Genre

A grasp of Mark's overriding reference to Scripture should keep the reader from regarding his Gospel as an eyewitness account or as any conventional form of biography or history. What Mark gives us is far richer. In keeping with the Jewish practices of his time, Mark interprets Jesus in the light of the Hebrew Bible. He uses Scripture as an interpretive framework. At the same time, he shows Jesus reinterpreting Scripture. Out of this two-way exchange, Mark offers us a Wisdom book.

Like other Wisdom books, Mark's Gospel derives its meaning from the Hebrew Bible. It takes place, for the most part, in the everyday settings of sea and synagogue, home and table. Its central figure, Jesus, offers wisdom in parables, riddles, and short pithy sayings called aphorisms. At the same time, Mark shows Jesus to be not only a teacher of Wisdom but Wisdom itself. Jesus calls his followers to an unconventional wisdom, a way of living (and a way of dying) that he himself exemplifies.

In modern terms, Mark's work is theological. As such, it is purposefully put together. An attentive reader cannot fail to notice Mark's craft: the repetition of certain significant words and the shaping of the narrative into symbolic events and meaningful patterns. There is a theological focus to his overall design.

Key words

Mark is given to the repetition of certain key words or phrases. Unfortunately, these key words and phrases are not always clear in our English translations. This commentary will provide a literal translation of these key words as it explores them throughout the Gospel, especially: "release," "rise up" or "be raised," "straightway," and "ecstasy."

Patterns and design

Mark shapes his narrative in patterns of twos and threes. The reader will be first aware of doublets. Sometimes this is a matter of repeating episodes; sometimes it is a matter of echoing words. There are, for example, two instances in Mark when Jesus calms the sea (chs. 4 and 6). Twice he multiplies bread for a hungry crowd (chs. 6 and 8). There are two occasions when people discuss who Jesus is (chs. 6 and 8). And there are numerous other examples, which this commentary will point out along the way.

At the end of chapter 8, Mark seems to give a reason for his method when he describes Jesus' healing of a blind man in two stages. Here he dramatizes the idea that the blind man cannot shift from darkness to vision all at once; he needs to go through a process of coming to sight. In the same way, careful readers will find that each repetition enlarges their understanding.

Mark also likes to pattern things in threes. There are three healing miracles, for example, in chapter 1, three questions asked of Jesus in chapter 2, three seed parables in chapter 4. Jesus makes three predictions of his death (in chs. 8, 9, and 10). As with the doublets, there are numerous other examples, which we will note as we go along. If readers become alert to this pattern, they will see that Mark always uses the middle of these triads to shed light on the other two.

Transfiguration at the center

Given Mark's careful choice of words and patterns, it is surely no accident that he places the scene of Jesus' transfiguration exactly in the middle of his Gospel (9:2). The transfiguration of Jesus is Mark's way of imaging his resurrection. The scene overshadows both parts of the Gospel, emphasizing God's creative, transforming, transfiguring power to restore life.

Mark's Gospel is sometimes called "the Gospel of the Cross," so it is worth noting that the transfiguration overshadows the cross. Mark arranges events so that the scene of transfiguration follows right after Jesus speaks to his disciples about taking up the cross, and it completes his meaning. Jesus says: "Whoever wishes to come after me must deny himself, take up his cross, and follow me. For whoever wishes to save his life will lose it, but whoever loses his life for my sake and that of the gospel will save it" (8:34-35). Mark does not explain this saying but dramatizes the paradox it contains by following this call to "lose" one's life with this scene of transfigured life. Mark does not show Jesus elevating the cross for its own sake, but rather embracing it as a means to transfiguration. In Mark, the whole teaching of Jesus is death-*and-resurrection*, cross-*and-transfiguration*.

Conclusion

Rich in Scripture, theological in purpose, and brilliant in design, Mark's Gospel invites its readers to become followers of Jesus' transfiguring wisdom.

NOTES ON THE TRANSLATION

Literal or root meanings

The Church encourages translators to return to "the original texts of the sacred books" (*The Dogmatic Constitution on Sacred Revelation*, 22). That recommendation has been followed scrupulously in this commentary, to the point where the commentator often renders the meaning of the biblical words and phrases in a more literal way than the NABRE translation provided. This kind of conscious choice, while found throughout the commentary in the author's own translations, is particularly evident in four key words that will be explored in the commentary: "release," "rise up" or "raised up," "straightway," and "ecstasy" or "ecstatic." These and other words translated by the author will be clearly marked with asterisks throughout the commentary.

Capitalization

In some instances, the difference between the commentator's translation and that of the NABRE involves capitalization. The reader should know that we have no original manuscripts of the Gospels, and that of those we do possess, the best were written entirely in capital letters called "uncials." Thus all modern capitals are the choice of a later editor. Such editorial emendations are, like translations, forms of interpretation. This commentator has chosen not to capitalize certain words in order to highlight what she believes to be Mark's theological view.

For example, she does not capitalize "son of man" because she believes that it is not used by Mark as a special title, but rather in its usual Hebrew sense of *ben 'adam*, which literally means "son of Adam" or "human being." (She also sees it as sometimes following the Aramaic custom of using it as an alternative to "I.") She believes that Mark's habit of constantly associating the term with Jesus expresses his theological perception of Jesus as a second Adam. She does not capitalize "messiah" because she wants to emphasize that Mark redefined that term in the process of using it, and she would like to encourage the reader to reflect on that redefinition. She does not capitalize "holy spirit" because she wants to remind the reader of its use throughout the Hebrew Bible. While the modern Christian of course sees this phrase in relation to the Trinitarian understanding of the fourth-century creed, Mark's first-century audience would have heard it in terms of the biblical tradition they knew.

Note: This Introduction has been abridged from the original introduction to this commentary found in the New Collegeville Bible Commentary, *The Gospel According to Mark*.

BEGINNING

Mark 1:1-45

1:1 Beginning

In the Greek text of Mark, the word "beginning" has nothing in front of it, neither "the" nor "a"; the Gospel starts abruptly with the simple word "Beginning." By this device Mark calls attention to this word and emphasizes it. In this way he recalls the opening of the Hebrew Bible—"In the beginning"—the moment of Creation. In Jewish tradition the word "beginning" was equated with Wisdom, because in the book of Proverbs personified Wisdom says, "The LORD begot me, *the beginning* of his works" (Prov 8:22). So some Jewish teachers paraphrased Genesis 1:1 to read, "In *Wisdom* God created the heavens and the earth." Mark's opening is thus rich in meaning, identifying the gospel (or "good news") of Jesus with Wisdom, and that Wisdom with a new Creation.

1:2-3 As it is written

Mark brings together here three voices from the Hebrew Scripture. The messenger who "goes ahead" suggests the angel God sent to lead his people to freedom in the story of the Exodus (23:20). The messenger sent to "prepare the way" suggests the figure whom God promises through the prophet Malachi and who will purge the people of their sins (Mal 3:1). The

I: The Preparation for the Public Ministry of Jesus

CHAPTER 1

1The beginning of the gospel of Jesus Christ [the Son of God].

The Preaching of John the Baptist

2As it is written in Isaiah the prophet:

"Behold, I am sending my messenger ahead
of you;
he will prepare your way.
3A voice of one crying out in the desert:
'Prepare the way of the Lord,
make straight his paths.'"

4John [the] Baptist appeared in the desert pro-
claiming a baptism of repentance for the forgive-
ness of sins. 5People of the whole Judean
countryside and all the inhabitants of Jerusalem
were going out to him and were being baptized
by him in the Jordan River as they acknowledged
their sins. 6John was clothed in camel's hair, with

continue

"voice of one crying out in the desert" is the herald described by Isaiah who is to give "comfort" to God's people (Isa 40:1). In just two verses Mark sums up a biblical tradition whereby angelic or human figures are sent to draw the people to God through preparation, through purgation, and through comfort. The messenger here is John the Baptist, who appears, in the next verse, as Isaiah's "voice . . . crying out in the desert."

1:4-8 John the Baptist

The description of John in 1:6 makes him resemble Elijah, who is similarly dressed in the Second Book of Kings (1:8). It was said that Elijah never died but ascended to heaven in a fiery chariot (2 Kgs 2:11). By interpreting John as another Elijah, Mark indicates John's greatness as a prophet. Elijah passed on his gift as a leather belt around his waist. He fed on locusts and wild honey. 7And this is what he proclaimed: "One mightier than I is coming after me. I am not worthy to stoop and loosen the thongs of his sandals. 8I have baptized you with water; he will baptize you with the holy Spirit."

The Baptism of Jesus

9It happened in those days that Jesus came from Nazareth of Galilee and was baptized in the Jordan by John. 10On coming up out of the water he saw the heavens being torn open and the Spirit, like a dove, descending upon him. 11And a voice came from the heavens, "You are my beloved Son; with you I am well pleased."

The Temptation of Jesus

12At once the Spirit drove him out into the desert, 13and he remained in the desert for forty days, tempted by Satan. He was among wild beasts, and the angels ministered to him.

continue

a prophet to a successor, Elisha; so here, Mark introduces John as a prophet who will be succeeded by another—Jesus. In the Elijah-Elisha stories, however, Elijah is pictured as the greater prophet; here, John's proclamation about Jesus reverses that order. The Elijah-Elisha context places Jesus in the tradition of the prophets, with their long habit of pressing for religious reform.

"A voice proclaims: / In the wilderness prepare the way of the LORD! / Make straight in the wasteland a highway for our God!" (Isa 40:3). How does this **quotation of Isaiah in Mark 1:2-3** differ from what was originally written in Isaiah? A footnote in the NABRE for Isaiah 40:3 states that in its original context, this verse was "a description of the return of the exiles from Babylon to Jerusalem (Zion)."

1:9-11 The baptism of Jesus

The scene that Mark portrays reinforces the idea that Creation is happening again: as in Genesis 1, God's spirit hovers over the waters. In describing the opening of the heavens, Mark uses an unusual word for that opening that means "rend"* or "split apart"*; he uses the word again near the end of his Gospel when he describes the splitting open of the sanctuary veil after Jesus' death (15:38). The echoing word links the two scenes, suggesting that Jesus is opening up God's dwelling place.

In a Jewish writing of the time *(The Testament of Judah)* the heavens are opened "to pour out the spirit as a blessing of the holy Father." Here God's spirit descends "like a dove," a term used for the beloved in the Song of Songs. The idea of God's beloved becomes explicit here in the "voice from the heavens" saying, "You are my beloved Son; with you I am well pleased."

The phrase "beloved Son" also brings to mind the story of Isaac, where God asks Abraham to "take your son, your only son, your beloved son" and offer him up as a sacrifice (Gen 22:2; author's translation). In ancient Passover liturgy, Isaac's sacrifice is referred to as a voluntary act on Isaac's part; Isaac merges with the Passover lamb as it is said that Isaac's blood was placed on the doorposts so that the angel of death would spare the Israelites. So the echo here points to Jesus' sacrificial death and its saving consequences.

1:12-13 Temptation in the desert

As the baptism scene recapitulates the opening of Genesis, so the reference to temptation for "forty days" in the desert encapsulates the key experience of Israel in the book of Exodus. There is no suggestion here, however, that Jesus' encounter with Satan involves a struggle. Rather, Mark gives us a static picture, the human figure of Jesus steadfast between "wild beasts" and ministering angels. It is an icon of original humanity, only this time not sinning.

*Author's own translation from the original Greek. In sections where the same words appear multiple times, only the first reference is noted.

1:14-15 "The gospel of God"

Jesus' ministry picks up where John's leaves off; "the gospel of God" suggests their continuity. While we tend to restrict the term "gospel" to the story of Jesus, Mark uses the term to refer to the broader narrative of all God's deeds among his people; it is the gospel or "good news" of God that both John and Jesus proclaim. Jesus, like John, calls the people to repentance. In both Greek and Hebrew the word translated here as "repent" carries the sense of "turning" or change of heart. Jesus calls people to this change not as a warning but as a promise: it is the "time of fulfillment," the time of God's "kingdom." In biblical thought, God's kingdom is not a particular place but a condition of living according to God's will. While it tends to be projected into the future, it can also denote a timeless state of being. Similarly, the "time of fulfillment" is not restricted to a particular moment but designates a realization of God's presence. Both these ideas are further unfolded in Mark's story.

II: The Mystery of Jesus

The Beginning of the Galilean Ministry

14 After John had been arrested, Jesus came to
Galilee proclaiming the gospel of God: 15 "This is
the time of fulfillment. The kingdom of God is at
hand. Repent, and believe in the gospel."

The Call of the First Disciples

16 As he passed by the Sea of Galilee, he saw
Simon and his brother Andrew casting their nets
into the sea; they were fishermen. 17 Jesus said to
them, "Come after me, and I will make you fishers
of men." 18 Then they abandoned their nets and
followed him. 19 He walked along a little farther
and saw James, the son of Zebedee, and his
brother John. They too were in a boat mending
their nets. 20 Then he called them. So they left their
father Zebedee in the boat along with the hired
men and followed him.

continue

The Greek word *metanoia*, used in **Jesus' call to "repent"** (Mark 1:15), literally means "to change one's mind." Pope Benedict XVI has noted that this Greek term is rich in layers of meaning, each of which helps us understand how this "change" should affect us as Christians. *Metanoia* calls us to reject past behaviors that are not in keeping with our new way of life, to make amends for those past behaviors whenever possible, and to reform our lives (see Joseph Cardinal Ratzinger, *Principles of Catholic Theology*). Thus for a Christian, the repentance Jesus requires is both a change of heart and a radical conversion that is manifested in action.

1:16-20 The call of the first disciples

In the ancient world, it was not customary for teachers to seek their disciples; on the contrary, teachers attracted disciples. Jesus' action here is therefore striking, for it suggests the action of personified Wisdom, who, in the book of Proverbs, does go about calling her followers. Wisdom calls those who are in need of her—the "simple ones" (Prov 1:22; NAB). So Jesus here calls simple fishermen. As Wisdom promises her followers a higher life, so Jesus promises his disciples that they will do a more advanced kind of "fishing."

The response of those called is equally striking. Without inquiry or hesitation, they leave both livelihood and family. Their quickness to respond is enhanced by a word omitted in most translations: Mark says that "*Straightway** they left their nets and followed him" (1:18). As we noted in the Introduction, the word "straightway" echoes the message of the voice crying in the desert, telling the people to prepare for God's coming by making "straight" his "ways" (1:3). The ready commitment of Simon and Andrew, James and John is thus shown to be the

The Cure of a Demoniac

[21]Then they came to Capernaum, and on the sabbath he entered the synagogue and taught. [22]The people were astonished at his teaching, for he taught them as one having authority and not as the scribes. [23]In their synagogue was a man with an unclean spirit; [24]he cried out, "What have you to do with us, Jesus of Nazareth? Have you come to destroy us? I know who you are—the Holy One of God!" [25]Jesus rebuked him and said, "Quiet! Come out of him!" [26]The unclean spirit convulsed him and with a loud cry came out of him. [27]All were amazed and asked one another, "What is this? A new teaching with authority. He commands even the unclean spirits and they obey him." [28]His fame spread everywhere throughout the whole region of Galilee.

The Cure of Simon's Mother-in-Law

[29]On leaving the synagogue he entered the house of Simon and Andrew with James and John. [30]Simon's mother-in-law lay sick with a fever. They immediately told him about her. [31]He approached, grasped her hand, and helped her up. Then the fever left her and she waited on them.

continue

ideal response of anyone called by God. It is worth noting that we never see any of these disciples make this ideal response again. Throughout most of Mark's Gospel they are singularly slow to understand or to follow Jesus. But Mark sets up this opening scene to suggest their ideal capabilities.

1:21-45 Three miracles of healing

Studies of the structure of Mark's Gospel have shown that he likes to link events, teachings, and sometimes words together in a pattern of three. When he does so, the middle event, teaching, or word always functions as the key one, shedding light on the other two. So here, at the conclusion of Mark's opening chapter, when we find three miracles of healing, it is important to notice how and for what purpose they are linked together.

1) The casting out of "an unclean spirit" (1:21-28). Although the NAB caption speaks of the "cure of a demoniac," Mark's text does not use the word "demon" here but "unclean spirit." The use of this term indicates the perception that possession by evil is an unnatural or pathological state, a perception that predominates in Mark's Gospel. In chapter 3, as we will see, Jesus implicitly contrasts possession by an unclean spirit with possession by God's holy spirit (3:29-30). Here in the synagogue, it is because he sees the man's natural state to be a holy one that Jesus heals the man by simply commanding the unclean spirit to leave him.

The unclean spirit, for its part, knows itself to be destroyed by the simple confrontation of "the Holy One of God" (1:24). It is significant that Jesus commands the unclean spirit to depart with the same word that he later uses to command the storm to "be still" (4:39).

The incident is enclosed in descriptions of the people's reaction to Jesus' power. They speak of his act of exorcism as "a new teaching" (1:27). Mark seems to imply that there is something new in Jesus' perception that possession by evil is reversible.

The word that Mark then chooses to describe the crowd's state at seeing the cure (here in verse 27 translated simply as "amazed") is also part of a pattern of three. Mark uses it again to describe the feelings of the crowd that sees Jesus immediately after his transfiguration (9:15) and again to describe Jesus' own disturbed emotions in Gethsemane (14:33). It might best be translated as a state of "shock" or enhanced consciousness.

An **exorcism** is a type of miracle story that relates the driving out of a demon from someone who is possessed (see also Mark 5:1-13; 9:14-29). Jesus' reputation for being an exorcist caused some to accuse him of being allied to demons or to the devil (Beelzebul), a charge that Jesus denies (Mark 3:22-27).

2) The raising up of Simon's mother-in-law (1:29-31). Short as this incident is, it is the middle and therefore key event of these three healings. Unfortunately, its full drama is obscured by the translation. The Greek word used to describe the woman's condition (1:30) is frequently used to describe someone already dead, and the Greek word used to describe her cure (1:31) is best translated "raised up."* (It is the same word used to describe Jesus' own resurrection in 16:6.) Finally, the phrase translated as "waited on them" would more accurately be rendered "served"* or "ministered to"* them (the Greek verb used is related to the word for "deacon"). So translated, the incident distills the essence of what Jesus is about: he takes a dead woman by the hand and raises her up, not only to new physical health but to a new spiritual status. Throughout the Gospel of Mark, Jesus says repeatedly that he has come "not to be served but to serve." This woman is the first person in the Gospel to act as Jesus does.

3) The healing of the leper (1:40-45). In his first miracle Jesus heals a man within the synagogue; here he heals a man who has been ostracized from the synagogue because of his illness. Jesus' relation to the synagogue here is complicated. On the one hand, by touching the leper he violates a religious prohibition against touching the "unclean"; on the other hand, Jesus sends the man back to the priests and the prescribed rituals for lepers. To complicate matters further, Jesus tells the healed man to "tell no one anything" (1:44) and yet suggests that the man's healed body will serve as a "proof" or "witness." And in fact the man does become a witness, spreading the word of Jesus' action. Jesus thus heals more than the man's body—he restores him to his community and changes him from someone who was alone and alienated to one who, it seems, cannot help bearing witness to God's healing power.

Other Healings

32 When it was evening, after sunset, they
brought to him all who were ill or possessed by
demons. 33 The whole town was gathered at the
door. 34 He cured many who were sick with various
diseases, and he drove out many demons, not permitting them to speak because they knew him.

Jesus Leaves Capernaum

35 Rising very early before dawn, he left and
went off to a deserted place, where he prayed.
36 Simon and those who were with him pursued
him 37 and on finding him said, "Everyone is looking for you." 38 He told them, "Let us go on to the
nearby villages that I may preach there also. For
this purpose have I come." 39 So he went into their
synagogues, preaching and driving out demons throughout the whole of Galilee.

The Cleansing of a Leper

40 A leper came to him [and kneeling down]
begged him and said, "If you wish, you can make
me clean." 41 Moved with pity, he stretched out his
hand, touched him, and said to him, "I do will it.
Be made clean." 42 The leprosy left him immediately,
and he was made clean. 43 Then, warning him sternly,
he dismissed him at once. 44 Then he said to him,

continue

Mark exhibits a curious feature that scholars have dubbed **"the messianic secret,"** or perhaps more accurately, "the secret of Jesus' identity." After some of his miracles, Jesus instructs the recipient(s) not to tell anyone (e.g., 1:44). They often abruptly ignore the command and spread the news of Jesus' miraculous ministry! This may be a literary technique to show how the characters in the story fail to fully comprehend the true goal of Jesus' ministry and the true nature of his messiahship. Jesus is destined to suffer and die on the cross, a destiny that was not expected of the coming messiah. It is not until Jesus' death that his identity can be understood, and it is revealed by the centurion (a Gentile) who stands at the foot of the cross: "Truly this man was the Son of God!" (15:39).

> "See that you tell no one anything, but go, show yourself to the priest and offer for your cleansing what Moses prescribed; that will be proof for them."
> 45 The man went away and began to publicize the whole matter. He spread the report abroad so that it was impossible for Jesus to enter a town openly. He remained outside in deserted places, and people kept coming to him from everywhere.

Summary of the healing miracles (1:21-45)

In the first instance, the unclean spirit within the man cries out upon being confronted by Jesus' holiness; in the second instance, friends bring Jesus to the woman who is sick; in this third incident, the sick man himself approaches Jesus and asks for help. Both the first and last healings involve bringing someone back to acceptance within the synagogue. In the first, Jesus touches uncleanness within; in the last, he touches uncleanness without.

The first and last healings involve people who, because they are considered "unclean," are forced to live on the fringe of Jewish religious society. What point, then, is Mark trying to make by placing the miracle of Simon's mother-in-law in between them? Is he not suggesting that the place of women in this society is on a par with them? The woman, it may be noted, does not even have a name; she is only known by her relationship to a man—in this case, not even her son but her son-in-law. Situated between a demoniac and a leper, the caricature of "the mother-in-law," we might guess, was an ancient joke. But Jesus, we have noted, not only cures her but changes her: he "raises her up."* By his use of this language, Mark signals to us that all of these miracles of healing are forerunners of Jesus' resurrection. Or to put it another way, Jesus' resurrection comprehends the raising up of all humanity.

1:32-39, 45b A rhythm of healing, preaching, and prayer

In between the healing of the mother-in-law and the leper, Mark tells us that Jesus continually healed the sick and drove out demons, and, when he could, withdrew to a deserted place to pray. Yet he also tells us that when Simon and others came to tell him that everyone was looking for him, he returned to the villages to preach, noting that this was his purpose. In this way, Mark indicates a tension in Jesus' life between outreach and withdrawal, or a rhythm of action and prayer. In the last part of the final verse, Mark suggests that this division collapses and that even in the desert Jesus is not away from the crowds that need healing.

Summary of chapter 1

In chapter 1, Mark sets out the framework for his whole Gospel: the traditions of Creation and Wisdom. He indicates that in Jesus, God is initiating a new beginning, a new creation. Through Jesus' connection with John and John's resemblance to Elijah, Mark suggests that Jesus is not, however, breaking off from Jewish tradition or the Jewish Bible but is acting in continuity with the prophets. Indeed, Mark suggests in many ways that Jesus is reenacting the history of Israel. In the scene of Jesus' baptism, Mark shows Jesus to be God's "beloved son," as Israel always named itself, and like Isaac, who also represents Israel in Jewish legend, to be a son destined for a sacrificial death that will be saving for many. Through the brief scene of Jesus' being tempted in the desert, Mark recalls the Israelites' experience of the Exodus.

Mark also shows that Jesus embodies the Wisdom traditions. Through his dramatization of Jesus' calling of his disciples, he suggests the figure of God's Wisdom calling the simple to be her followers. Through his presentation of Jesus as a healer, Mark expands upon the idea of Wisdom as one who seeks to restore God's creation. Although Mark describes Jesus as teaching and preaching, what he actually shows us is Jesus totally given over to making people whole. Through the language of "raising up"* in a key miracle, Mark indicates that he sees resurrection as the ultimate act of Wisdom's way of restoration or re-creation.

EXPLORING LESSON ONE

1. What do we know about the authorship of Mark and its intended audience?

2. What are some of the ways themes from the Old Testament are employed by Mark and associated with Jesus?

3. Why is it important to read the Gospel of Mark as something other than a biography of Jesus?

4. How does Mark's use of "beginning" in Mark 1:1 echo the Old Testament?

5. How does Mark's depiction of John the Baptist identify John as a prophet (1:4-8)?

6. What connection is there between Jesus' baptism (1:9-11) and the creation account in Genesis 1:1-2?

7. As brief as Mark's account of Jesus' temptation is (1:12-13), what gives it a rich association with the book of Exodus? (See Exod 16:2-3.)

8. Read again the account Mark gives of Jesus calling his disciples (1:16-20). When have you sensed, or in what ways do you now sense, God's call in your life?

9. a) Of the three healings in Mark 1:21-45, which one does the commentary discuss as the key healing? Why is it key?

   b) Which one of these healing stories resonates most with you? Why is it meaningful to you?

10. In Mark 1:35-39 we see Jesus pursuing solitude in prayer as well as active engagement with others. How do you balance action and contemplation in your own spiritual life?

CLOSING PRAYER

Prayer

"You are my beloved Son; with you I am well pleased." (Mark 1:11)

Jesus, beloved of God, mold us and fashion us so that our lives reflect your goodness, your truth, and your healing presence. We pray this day for those we love, including . . .

LESSON TWO

Mark 2–3

Begin your personal study and group discussion with a simple and sincere prayer such as:

Prayer

Loving God, open my mind and heart to hear your voice. Increase my understanding and inspire in me a greater desire to follow Jesus.

Read the Bible text of Mark 2–3 found in the outside columns of pages 28–39, highlighting what stands out to you.

Read the accompanying commentary to add to your understanding.

Respond to the questions on pages 40–41, Exploring Lesson Two.

The Closing Prayer on page 42 is for your personal use and may be used at the end of group discussion.

CHAPTER 2

The Healing of a Paralytic

[1]When Jesus returned to Capernaum after some days, it became known that he was at home. [2]Many gathered together so that there was no longer room for them, not even around the door, and he preached the word to them. [3]They came bringing to him a paralytic carried by four men. [4]Unable to get near Jesus because of the crowd, they opened up the roof above him. After they had broken through, they let down the mat on which the paralytic was lying. [5]When Jesus saw their faith, he said to the paralytic, "Child, your sins are forgiven." [6]Now some of the scribes were sitting there asking themselves, [7]"Why does this man speak that way? He is blaspheming. Who

continue

JESUS' ACTS OF RESTORATION AND RE-CREATION

Mark 2:1-28

2:1-4 Breaking through the roof

As chapter 1 concludes with the description of a crowd coming to Jesus even in "deserted places," so chapter 2 opens with so many people gathered in Jesus' home that "there was no longer room for them, not even around the door" (2:2). As a consequence, Mark tells us, the four friends bringing a paralytic to Jesus resort to opening up the roof above him (2:2-4). Although the vocabulary is not identical, there is an interesting parallel here to the heavens opening up at Jesus' baptism; it is typical of Mark's theological slant to suggest that Jesus continually opens things up. In the rest of this chapter, Mark shows Jesus opening up new meanings in sinfulness and forgiveness.

2:5-7 "Your sins are released"

It is in keeping with this view that Mark shows Jesus telling the paralytic that his sins are "released"* or "let go."* The word is not translated that way because it is not idiomatic English, but it is literally correct and more accurately reflects Mark's view that evil binds but God sets free. The same verb is used by Mark to describe John's baptism "for the *release** of sins" (1:4), the action of Simon and Andrew in *letting go** of their nets (1:18), and the fever *letting go* of Simon's mother-in-law when Jesus raises her up (1:31).

2:6-7 "Who but God alone can forgive sins?"

This reflection of the scribes is sometimes taken as Markan irony—that is, it is suggested that by phrasing it the way he does, Mark makes the challenge of the scribes unwittingly point to Jesus' special and divine powers. But another possible interpretation is that Mark is making the scribes raise an old theological question so that he can then show Jesus answering it in an unconventional way. When we read the Gospels as eyewitness accounts, we often miss the carefully constructed rhetorical patterns common in the ancient world. It is worth reflecting that from Plato on, it was a common teaching technique to construct a dialogue between a master teacher and an obtuse listener; the questions of the obtuse listener serve to draw out the thought of the master teacher. So here, the question of the scribes serves as a catalyst for Jesus' teaching on forgiveness. And Jesus teaches more than once in Mark's Gospel that human beings are called to forgive one another in imitation of God's forgiveness of them. If one argues to the contrary that only God can forgive, one could use this idea to dodge the obligation to forgive others.

2:9 "Which is easier to say . . . ?"

In typical Jewish fashion, Jesus often answers a question with a question. The question he raises here is something of a riddle, for while forgiving sins is clearly the harder thing to do, it is by far the easier thing to say because it requires no visible proof. (No one can check on whether or not sins have been forgiven, but the cure of paralyzed limbs is either seen or not seen.)

By means of quoting this riddle, Mark also suggests that Jesus equates the act of forgiveness with the act of healing—that is, he shows that Jesus taught that to forgive someone is to heal them. Mark thus implies that all of Jesus' acts of healing are theological symbols of God's desire to forgive us and make us whole. The miracles of healing have a theological dimension.

In the ancient world, moreover, people often believed (as indeed, some people still do) that illness or injury was a punishment inflicted by God for some sin. By coupling forgiveness with healing, Mark shows how Jesus taught that it is God's will to forgive rather than to punish, to heal rather than to hurt.

2:10 "The son of man"

What does Jesus mean by saying that "the Son of Man has authority to forgive sins on earth"? Many scholars have noted that in Mark, "the son of man" is the way Jesus most often refers to himself; they have then interpreted this phrase as a special title. But recent scholarship has pointed out that in Hebrew and Aramaic the phrase simply means "human being," as in Psalm 8:5:

> What is man that you are mindful of him,
> and a *son of man* that you care for him?

> but God alone can forgive sins?" 8Jesus immediately knew in his mind what they were thinking to themselves, so he said, "Why are you thinking such things in your hearts? 9Which is easier, to say to the paralytic, 'Your sins are forgiven,' or to say, 'Rise, pick up your mat and walk'? 10But that you may know that the Son of Man has authority to forgive sins on earth"—11he said to the paralytic, "I say to you, rise, pick up your mat, and go home." 12He rose, picked up his mat at once, and went away in the sight of everyone.
>
> *continue*

It has also been noted that in Aramaic the phrase was often used as a form of self-reference. Still others note that in Hebrew the phrase literally equals "son of Adam." All these facts suggest that in using it, Mark was not giving Jesus a special title but rather emphasizing his common humanity. If he attaches any special role to it, it is not that of apocalyptic agent but rather that of second Adam, a representative of humanity giving us all a fresh start.

When Mark quotes Jesus saying that "the Son of Man has authority to forgive sins on earth," he seems to be suggesting that all human beings have the power to forgive and that Jesus as the second Adam is modeling this role for all of us. This function of the phrase "son of man" needs to be kept in mind when we see it again at the end of this chapter (2:27).

2:11-12a "Rise, pick up your mat, and go home"

Once again Mark chooses the same verb for "rise up"* in a healing miracle that he will use to describe the raising up of Jesus. The immediate response of the paralytic is intensified in Mark's text by the additional word "straightway"*; the straightening of the man's limbs is presented as one more instance of "making straight the way of the LORD."

They were all astounded and glorified God, saying, "We have never seen anything like this."

The Call of Levi

[13]Once again he went out along the sea. All the crowd came to him and he taught them. [14]As he passed by, he saw Levi, son of Alphaeus, sitting at the customs post. He said to him, "Follow me."

continue

2:12b "They were all astounded . . ."

The word translated here as "astounded" is literally "out of their minds"* or ecstatic. This response of the crowd is echoed in the later response of those who witness the raising up of a little girl (5:42) and, at the very end of the Gospel, in the response of the three women who come to realize the implications of the empty tomb (16:8). The experience of being ecstatic thus forms a pattern in Mark. Its implications need further exploring.

2:13-17 The calling of tax collectors and sinners

This is the second time in Mark's Gospel that Jesus calls disciples to himself; there will be a third calling in chapter 3. The calling of disciples is thus a Markan triad, and knowing the pattern, we can anticipate that the middle incident—which is this one—will be key, shedding light on the meaning of the other two. We have seen that in the first, the disciples respond in ideal fashion ("straightway"). In the third calling (3:13-19), Jesus not only calls disciples to himself but sends them out "to preach and . . . to drive out demons" (3:14-15). We are also given the names of the twelve apostles, including that of Jesus' betrayer. In this middle incident, Mark dramatizes the fact that Jesus calls not saints but sinners.

2:13-14 Levi

The first to be called is Levi, "sitting at the customs post." To understand the implications of this call and why Levi would have been regarded as a public sinner, it is necessary to know something of the history of the Jerusalem Temple and the Jewish priesthood in the time of Jesus and of Mark.

From the eighth century before the time of Jesus until the time of the Gospels, every major power in the Mediterranean world conquered the Jews and occupied Jerusalem: Assyria, Babylon, Persia, Greece, and Rome. Babylon destroyed Solomon's Temple in the sixth century. Under the Persian king Cyrus, the Jews were allowed to rebuild it. In the first century, Herod expanded it, but the Romans destroyed it again in the year 70. Both the Greeks and the Romans were especially hostile to the Jewish faith because they felt that it detracted from their secular power. The Greeks under Alexander III began to undermine the power of the Temple by appointing the high priests. No longer was the priesthood the sacred legacy of Aaron, no longer was it handed down to the special tribe of Levi. It became a political appointment, a job up for sale like any other appointment in the world of power and money.

The most anti-Jewish of the Greek rulers was a man named Antiochus IV. His attempt to wipe out Judaism through the banning of circumcision together with acts of sacrilege in the Temple occasioned the revolt of the Maccabees (whose victory and purifying of the Temple is still celebrated each year at Hanukkah). At the time of Jesus and of Mark, the Romans had taken up where the Greeks left off. They continued the practice of appointing the high priests, and they also attempted to desecrate the Temple in other ways.

In this context, tax collectors were hated, not just because they took money but because they took it from the Jewish people for the benefit of Rome. Levi, "sitting at his customs post," is an apt symbol of the Roman corruption of the Jewish priesthood. Instead of being a religious leader as Levites had originally been destined, this Levi has sold out to the enemy and collects taxes for them.

Tax collectors in the ancient world did not have the best reputations. They were known for extortion and were often ostracized socially and religiously. When Jesus spoke with Levi, he responded in two ways: he followed Jesus, and he provided a meal for him. Sharing a meal is an intrinsically social thing to do. Food is given as a gift; time is involved in preparation and in the mealtime itself; conversation is a natural part of the experience. Jesus was often criticized for eating with sinners and tax collectors—those who were on the fringes of society—because of the social connections that eating together indicated. And maybe that all began with one tax collector who was addressed as a person rather than a social outcast: one tax collector who hosted a meal where Jesus was a guest, and where sinners were welcome at the table.

And he got up and followed him.
15 While he was at table in his house, many tax collectors and sinners sat with Jesus and his disciples; for there were many who followed him.
16 Some scribes who were Pharisees saw that he was eating with sinners and tax collectors and said to his disciples, "Why does he eat with tax collectors and sinners?"
17 Jesus heard this and said to them [that], "Those who are well do not need a physician, but the sick do. I did not come to call the righteous but sinners."

The Question about Fasting

18 The disciples of John and of the Pharisees were accustomed to fast. People came to him and objected, "Why do the disciples of John and the disciples of the Pharisees fast, but your disciples do not fast?"
19 Jesus answered them, "Can the wedding guests fast while the bridegroom is with them? As long as they have the bridegroom with

continue

2:15-28 Three questions of Wisdom

1) "Why does he eat with tax collectors and sinners?" (2:16-17). Modern readers sometimes regard this question as one that reveals the Pharisees' legalism and rigidity, but we should recognize it instead as one that is not unnatural for any pious member of a religious community. We might ask ourselves: How readily would today's churchgoers welcome an enemy collaborator into their midst? It also helps our understanding to realize that because the dietary laws were well defined in Judaism, eating with non-Jews was complicated and potentially an occasion for religious backsliding. The question, then, does not reflect so badly on the Pharisees; yet Jesus' response does emphasize his radical inclusiveness.

Jesus' response ("Those who are well do not need a physician, but the sick do," 2:17) is designed by Mark to reveal more of his identity. His reply here is the kind of pithy aphorism that one finds in the book of Proverbs and other Wisdom writings. By showing Jesus speaking in this style, Mark is dramatizing Jesus as a teacher of Wisdom. Even more, when he quotes Jesus as saying, "I did not come to call the righteous but sinners," he is placing Jesus in the role of Wisdom herself, who seeks out all those who have need of her, especially the unwise or the sinner.

Modern readers sometimes interpret Jesus' statement by saying that he really meant the "*self*-righteous." How, they think, could he possibly exclude the righteous? But their thinking betrays a certain literalism. If we realize that Mark is intent upon presenting Jesus to us as God's Wisdom incarnate, then we can hear these words, not as those of an ordinary religious leader, but as the speech of Wisdom herself—Wisdom seeking out the foolish sinner.

2) Feasting or fasting? (2:18-22). The second question asked of Jesus here comes not from the Pharisees but from the people. The question is typical of all people who have made them they cannot fast. [20]But the days will come when the bridegroom is taken away from them, and then they will fast on that day. [21]No one sews a piece of unshrunken cloth on an old cloak. If he does, its fullness pulls away, the new from the old, and the tear gets worse. [22]Likewise, no one pours new wine into old wineskins. Otherwise, the wine will burst the skins, and both the wine and the skins are ruined. Rather, new wine is poured into fresh wineskins."

The Disciples and the Sabbath

[23]As he was passing through a field of grain on the sabbath, his disciples began to make a path while picking the heads of grain. [24]At this the

continue

a religious commitment, because it is natural for pious folk to assume that there is a right way and a wrong way of doing things. If they see two religious leaders whom they respect doing things differently, they naturally want to know which one is right. Jesus' indirect reply (again a question answered by a question) suggests that there are no absolutes here but simply seasons of appropriateness. His response is again reminiscent of the Wisdom writings—this time, of Ecclesiastes:

> There is an appointed time for everything. . . .
> A time to weep, and a time to laugh;
> a time to mourn, and a time to dance
> (Eccl 3:1, 4).

The point is bolstered by two more Wisdom sayings: "No one sews a piece of unshrunken cloth on an old cloak" (2:21) and "No one pours new wine into old wineskins" (2:22).

Like so many of the concise truths of Proverbs, these sayings are homey, seeming to arise from close observation in a domestic setting. They are not in themselves profound, but they support the perspective implicit in the reply about fasting or feasting that there are seasons in the spiritual life. This pair of sayings also suggests that there can be a tension if we try to force a new style upon an old one.

Many Christians have been tempted to read in here a contrast between the "Old Testament" and the New Testament or between Judaism and Christianity, but such contrasts would have made no sense to Mark. At the time Mark was composing, there was no division between testaments; what we now call the "Old" or First Testament constituted all the Scripture there was. There was, moreover, not yet an established Christian church that sharply distinguished itself from Judaism. So the tension between "old" and "new" here cannot be taken as a Jewish-Christian conflict; it is simply a wise observation about the unsettling effects of new patterns upon old ones. It is worth noting, moreover, that Jesus suggests here that his disciples will eventually and appropriately return to fasting (2:20). The time of the bridegroom is not here permanently—at least, not yet.

The image of the bridegroom suggests the Song of Songs as well as the marriage feast between God and humanity described in Isaiah, some of the other prophets, and some of the psalms. The new clothing and the new wine go along with the image of this feasting. Through this series of aphorisms Mark seems to be suggesting two different time frames—one present and one future. Jesus as "bridegroom" anticipates humanity's future with God, and to the extent that his followers perceive him as such, they feast in the light of this future promise. But that future has not yet arrived, and the dissonance between that future promise and the present reality is experienced as the tension of new cloth pulling at old or new wine causing familiar containers to burst open.

3) "Why are they doing what is unlawful on the sabbath?" (2:23-28). The third question comes like the first from the Pharisees, and also like the first, it expresses moral outrage. This time the outrage comes from Jesus' direct violation of the Sabbath laws, which forbade all work of any kind, from picking grain to cooking it. Modern Christian readers tend to dismiss these laws as superficial and again condemn the Pharisees as legalists. But the Sabbath laws were designed to foreshadow the end time, when, according to God's promise, there would be no work, no war, no illness, and no distinctions in authority and power, but all—male and female, slave and free—would sit down together as equals at God's banquet and share in God's rest. This "rest" was not conceived of as the mere absence of work but as a joyous sharing in God's timeless presence. One did not heal on the Sabbath because symbolically the Sabbath was a time without illness.

Once again Mark uses a question that gives him the opportunity to set forth Jesus' teaching on the Sabbath. Jesus' teaching indirectly reminds the Pharisees that the essential purpose of the Sabbath is to anticipate and celebrate the wholeness for which God originally created human beings. Thus, he implies, satisfying human hunger is more in keeping with the purpose of the Sabbath than all the rules and rituals, even the sacred bread.

Jesus' final saying, "The sabbath was made for man, not man for the sabbath," sums up this idea of original humanity as the apex of God's creation. The final saying, "The Son of Man is lord even of the sabbath," should thus not be taken to mean that only Jesus is lord of the Sabbath; rather, it summarizes Jesus' role throughout the Gospel of Mark as the second Adam, the representative of humanity restored to its original wholeness. It is saying that God made the Sabbath for human beings as a symbol of their final destiny—a love feast with him and with one another.

Jewish Sabbath observances are based on God's command to keep the **Sabbath day** "holy" (Exod 20:8; Deut 5:12). A comprehensive definition of what constitutes the "work" that cannot be performed on the Sabbath, however, is not made explicit in the Torah. "Plowing and harvesting" (Exod 34:21) are clearly forbidden on the Sabbath as is the collection of firewood (Num 15:32-36) and the lighting of fires (Exod 35:3). But

Pharisees said to him, "Look, why are they doing what is unlawful on the sabbath?" [25]He said to them, "Have you never read what David did when he was in need and he and his companions were hungry? [26]How he went into the house of God when Abiathar was high priest and ate the bread of offering that only the priests could lawfully eat, and shared it with his companions?" [27]Then he said to them, "The sabbath was made for man, not man for the sabbath. [28]That is why the Son of Man is lord even of the sabbath."

continue

questions have remained about the permissibility of many other activities. Over the centuries, Jewish oral tradition has developed numerous laws that describe in very specific detail what work can or cannot be undertaken on the Sabbath so that devout Jews can be confident that they are complying with God's Sabbath directive.

Summary of chapter 2

In chapter 2, Mark dramatizes the way that Jesus, like Wisdom, restores human beings to wholeness, both physical and spiritual. In the opening incident, he shows Jesus equating forgiveness with healing. He next shows Jesus, again like Wisdom, seeking out sinners to be his followers. In particular, he shows Jesus singling out Levi, who stands for all the Jewish religious leaders who were selling out to Rome and thus weakening Jewish faith. By calling him to be his follower, Jesus/Wisdom is implicitly calling him, and Israel in general, to turn away from worldly power and back to the wisdom of their fathers.

Mark then sets up three questions asked of Jesus by perplexed people around him. These questions give Mark the opportunity to set forth Jesus' teaching on sin and forgiveness, religious behavior, and the purpose of the Sabbath. Mark shows Jesus responding in the style of Wisdom, both in terms of his aphoristic speech and in terms of his active seeking out of those who need him. The middle question about fasting or feasting gives Mark the opportunity to indicate the tension Jesus causes by his unconventional ways and how that unconventionality is the result of Jesus' anticipation of the future of humanity, when humankind, restored to original wholeness, will be gathered at the marriage feast of God. By means of the final question, Mark sets forth Jesus' teaching on the Sabbath. In his response Jesus teaches that the Sabbath was created for the benefit of humanity and as a sign and foretaste of its eternal banquet with the divine.

By these means, Mark develops the themes of Wisdom and Creation he introduced in the first chapter. In the second chapter he shows Jesus acting and speaking like God's Wisdom, God's co-creator in Proverbs (Prov 8:30), restoring people to wholeness, unsettling people from their familiar ways, and teaching that human wholeness is central to God's purpose.

JESUS' CHALLENGE OF CONVENTIONAL WISDOM

Mark 3:1-35

3:1-3 Healing the man with a withered hand

The image of something "withered" is a repeated one in Mark; it is part of his Creation theme, contrasting the withering of created things with their intended fruitfulness. In chapter 4, for example, the seed sown in shallow soil withers up (4:6); in chapter 9, "withering away" is one of the effects of an unclean spirit (9:18; translated as "becomes rigid" in the NABRE); in chapter 11, it becomes one of the seasons of the cursed fig tree (11:20-21).

In curing this man's withered arm, Jesus is acting out the restorative role of God the Creator, a role usually assigned to God's Wisdom. Jesus' first act here is to ask the man to "rise up"* (a resurrection word again) and to come forward "into the midst"* of the community. The implication is that the withered arm of the man had alienated him (like the leper) from the religious community, or at least put him on the fringes of it. Jesus' action here thus defies the conventional shunning of the physically disabled; it is doubly restorative.

3:4-5 The purpose of the Sabbath

This scene of healing is also used by Mark as an extension of Jesus' teaching on the Sabbath. Mark implies that many who witnessed this healing in the synagogue were once again more concerned about the Sabbath rules than about the purpose of the Sabbath. He shows Jesus challenging them explicitly: "Is it lawful to do good on the sabbath rather than to do evil, to save life rather than to destroy it?" (3:4). The large and absolute terms Jesus uses here seem to echo the moment in Deuteronomy when God sets before his people the large issues of life and death: "I have set before you life and death. . . . Choose life, then, that you and your descendants may live" (Deut 30:19). Jesus' question here, in other words, is framed so as to echo this proclamation of God. His argument is clearly not a small one over specific rules but a large one over the purpose of human worship.

Mark goes on to describe Jesus as "looking around them with anger and grieved at their hardness of heart" (3:5a). This particular mixture of anger and grief is also reminiscent of God's feelings as they are frequently portrayed in the Hebrew Bible. God is not portrayed there as unmoved and immovable, but as loving, jealous, angry, grieving, and forgiving. "Hardness of heart," on the other hand—the unmoved and immovable heart—is a common phrase the Hebrew Bible uses to express the human condition of sinfulness.

Further, when Mark shows Jesus in the actual act of curing the man, he quotes him as saying, "Stretch out your hand" (3:5b), a phrase that echoes the moment in Exodus when God tells Moses to stretch forth his hand over the sea to prepare a path for the Israelites' escape (Exod 14:16). The echo here is evocative, suggesting that Jesus not only cures the arm but gives the man new freedom. In all these different ways, Mark describes Jesus as a reflection of God.

3:6 The Pharisees and the Herodians

Mark sets up these two groups as particularly in opposition to Jesus. It is a surprising combination. The Pharisees were laypeople and scholars of the Bible. In spite of their later Christian reputation, they were in fact flexible interpreters of Scripture, believers in resurrection, and devoted to the cause of bringing Temple holiness into the home. The Herodians, on the other hand, were nominally Jews, but, in practice, collaborators with Rome; they were successively appointed by Rome to be tetrarchs of Palestine. The Romans called each tetrarch "the king of the Jews." The Herodians were obvious opponents of Jesus, but the Pharisees were not. Some scholars have even wondered if Jesus is shown arguing so much with the Pharisees because he belonged generally to their school of thought.

It is worth noting that the Pharisees do not show up again in Mark's description of Jesus' arrest and death. Judas makes his deal with "the chief priests" (14:10), with whom the Pharisees were not connected. It is true that the Pharisees do reappear with the Herodians here, trying to entrap Jesus by their question about paying taxes to Caesar (12:13). Yet Mark, more than any other evangelist, seems to implicate Rome in Jesus' death. We know that Matthew's anger against the Pharisees is directed not to those of Jesus' time but to those of Matthew's day who were putting the Jewish followers of Jesus out of the synagogues. It is possible that the same phenomenon accounts for their characterization here. Thematically, of course, the plotting of Jesus' death signals their negative response to the choice set before them between death and life.

CHAPTER 3

A Man with a Withered Hand

[1]Again he entered the synagogue. There was a man there who had a withered hand. [2]They watched him closely to see if he would cure him on the sabbath so that they might accuse him. [3]He said to the man with the withered hand, "Come up here before us." [4]Then he said to them, "Is it lawful to do good on the sabbath rather than to do evil, to save life rather than to destroy it?" But they remained silent. [5]Looking around at them with anger and grieved at their hardness of heart, he said to the man, "Stretch out your hand." He stretched it out and his hand was restored. [6]The Pharisees went out and immediately took counsel with the Herodians against him to put him to death.

The Mercy of Jesus

[7]Jesus withdrew toward the sea with his disciples. A large number of people [followed] from Galilee and from Judea. [8]Hearing what he was doing, a large number of people came to him also from Jerusalem, from Idumea, from beyond the Jordan, and from the neighborhood of Tyre and Sidon. [9]He told his disciples to have a boat ready for him because of the crowd, so that they would not crush him. [10]He had cured many and, as a result, those who had diseases were pressing upon him to touch him. [11]And whenever unclean spirits saw him they would fall down before him and

continue

3:7-10 The crowds that follow Jesus

In between key episodes and teachings, Mark interweaves passages about the crowds that follow Jesus. These passages serve to balance the picture of a few Jewish leaders plotting against Jesus with the picture of the large Jewish crowds who push to be close to him.

3:11 The unclean spirits that proclaim Jesus "Son of God"

Throughout the Gospel of Mark, the unclean spirits recognize Jesus' holiness, and even before he commands them to leave, they

shout, "You are the Son of God." 12He warned
them sternly not to make him known.

The Mission of the Twelve

13He went up the mountain and summoned
those whom he wanted and they came to him.
14He appointed twelve [whom he also named
apostles] that they might be with him and he
might send them forth to preach 15and to have
authority to drive out demons: 16[he appointed
the twelve:] Simon, whom he named Peter;
17James, son of Zebedee, and John the brother of
James, whom he named Boanerges, that is, sons
of thunder; 18Andrew, Philip, Bartholomew, Matthew,
Thomas, James the son of Alphaeus; Thaddeus,
Simon the Cananean, 19and Judas Iscariot
who betrayed him.

continue

feel instantly displaced by his presence. We have already heard one such spirit cry out, "What have you to do with us, Jesus of Nazareth? Have you come to destroy us?" (1:24). It is part of Mark's irony that he shows the unclean spirits to have such clarity about Jesus' identity, while he shows the human followers of Jesus to be confused and uncertain. The fact that Mark shows them calling Jesus "Son of God" should not be taken as a proclamation of Jesus' role in the Trinity, because that doctrinal formulation was not arrived at until the fourth century. Rather, Mark is indicating that the spirit world saw Jesus clearly as God's image. (There is an early Jewish tradition that when God showed the angels the first human being, they saw God's reflection so clearly that they knelt in worship.)

The title **"Son of God"** was often used in the ancient Near East as a title of kingship. In the Old Testament, similar use of the title can be found in the psalms (Pss 2:7; 89:26-27) and in the description of God's relationship with the descendant of David who would reign over a never-ending kingdom: "I will be a father to him, and he shall be a son to me" (2 Sam 7:14). While the Gospel of Mark frequently refers to Jesus as the Son of God (1:1; 3:11; 5:7; 15:39), an understanding of the title "Son of God" as an acknowledgment of Jesus' divinity developed over time in the early church and was confirmed through a series of decrees issued by church councils (Nicaea, Ephesus, and Chalcedon) in the fourth and fifth centuries C.E.

3:12 "He warned them sternly not to make him known"

Much has been made by some readers of Mark over the repeated way he shows Jesus trying to silence those who recognize his holiness. This has been interpreted by some to mean that Jesus wanted to keep his identity hidden, and this theory is referred to in some books as "the messianic secret." But such an interpretation assumes that Mark is simply recording what Jesus said and did; it gives no credit to Mark as a shaping author and theologian. If, on the contrary, we assume that Mark has a theological purpose in mind, then we will hear these admonitions to silence differently. They serve two theological functions. First, by showing Jesus repeatedly asking others not to talk about his holiness or his ability to heal, Mark sets Jesus off from the typical hero who demands recognition of his powers. Second, Mark makes the spread of Jesus' reputation even more significant because it grows in spite of him.

3:13-19 The third calling of disciples

As the last of a triad, this calling should be read in connection with the other two (1:16-20; 2:13-17). As we noted before, in the first calling episode, the disciples appear to be saints responding in an ideal way, but in the second calling scene, it is clear that Jesus is seeking out sinners. This time Mark expands upon the scene by suggesting the purpose of Jesus' calling and by giving us the names of those called. Mark tells us that Jesus "appointed twelve" in order that "he might send them forth to preach and to have authority [or power] to drive out demons." When Mark describes Jesus ascending a mountain to do this, he evokes the memory of Moses; when he emphasizes the number twelve, he evokes the twelve tribes of Israel. He thus implies that Jesus' gathering and sending forth of twelve followers is an act in continuity with Jewish tradition. The actions of preaching and casting out of demons are in continuity with the prophets.

Some of the names of the twelve are also significant. Peter, James, and John are the three whom Jesus will take to see the raising up of a child (5:37), his transfiguration (9:2), and his distress in Gethsemane (14:33). They also are given different names, always a signal in the Hebrew Bible of an inner transformation. Yet at the end we are also given the name of his betrayer. So Mark, in giving us a list of names, is giving us more than practical information. He is confirming what he suggested in the first two calling episodes, namely, that Jesus' disciples are a mixed lot, with one who would ultimately betray him and others who would ultimately be transformed by him. The reappearance of these four in other episodes of Mark's Gospel is worth tracking.

In secular usage in the ancient world, the term **apostle** (from the Greek *apostolos*, meaning "one sent forth") was originally used in the context of seafaring and referred to the dispatch of a fleet or a naval expedition. In the New Testament, the word is most often used to refer to the twelve chosen by Jesus to be his closest companions and to proclaim the gospel. The designation of "apostle" is also applied to others in the New Testament such as Paul, who witnessed the risen Christ and received a commission to preach in his name.

Blasphemy of the Scribes

[20]He came home. Again [the] crowd gathered,
making it impossible for them even to eat. [21]When
his relatives heard of this they set out to seize him,
for they said, "He is out of his mind." [22]The scribes
who had come from Jerusalem said, "He is possessed by Beelzebul," and "By the prince of demons he drives out demons."

Jesus and Beelzebul

[23]Summoning them, he began to speak to them
in parables, "How can Satan drive out Satan? [24]If
a kingdom is divided against itself, that kingdom
cannot stand. [25]And if a house is divided against
itself, that house will not be able to stand. [26]And
if Satan has risen up against himself and is divided, he cannot stand; that is the end of him.

continue

3:20-21 "He is out of his mind"

Once again Mark links episodes with a comment about the crowds pressing in on Jesus, this time to the point where no one could eat. Mark then comments that Jesus' relatives (literally, "those who were close to him," so perhaps his disciples) "set out to seize him, for they said, 'He is out of his mind.'" The Greek word that is translated "out of his mind" literally means "out of himself"; it is related to the Greek word for "ecstasy," on which we have commented before (see 2:12b). By using it, Mark suggests that Jesus has a more heightened consciousness than those around him.

3:22-30 Satan, forgiveness, and the holy spirit

By quoting the protests of the scribes to Jesus' exorcisms, Mark presents more of Jesus' teaching on forgiveness. The scribes say that Jesus himself must be possessed by Satan in order to drive out demons. Implicit in their statement is the idea that good and evil are so distinct and opposite that the "good" person should not go anywhere near "evil" persons.

27But no one can enter a strong man's house to
plunder his property unless he first ties up the
strong man. Then he can plunder his house.
28Amen, I say to you, all sins and all blasphemies
that people utter will be forgiven them. 29But who-
ever blasphemes against the holy Spirit will never
have forgiveness, but is guilty of an everlasting sin."
30For they had said, "He has an unclean spirit."

continue

This thought is a logical extension of the idea that if Jesus were truly a person of God, he would not eat with sinners.

Jesus refutes this point of view in several ways. First he asks the common sense question, "How can Satan drive out Satan?" He goes on to make the observation that a kingdom divided against itself cannot stand (3:23-24). Next he uses the analogy of "the strong man": "But no one can enter a strong man's house to plunder his property unless he first ties up the strong man. Then he can plunder his house" (3:27). Some interpretations of this analogy assert that "the strong man" is Satan, and Jesus is the one who ties him up. But this would turn Jesus into a plunderer as well as a violent enforcer of his will—roles that violate everything we know of Jesus' teachings. Rather, it makes more sense to see that the violent intruder is Satan, and "the strong man" is the normally good person who is bound and robbed by him.

This view is borne out by Jesus' final words here about forgiveness—that "all sins and all blasphemies" will be forgiven except the blasphemy against the holy spirit (3:29). What Jesus means by "the sin against the holy Spirit" has been puzzled over for centuries. The problem probably arose from capitalizing "holy spirit" and then assuming that "the sin against the Holy Spirit" was a special offense. But Mark would not have been thinking in terms of a Trinitarian formula. He would have been using "holy spirit" to mean simply God's spirit, as it appears in Psalm 51:13:

Do not drive me from before your face,
nor take from me your holy spirit.

The clue to Jesus' meaning here lies in the final explanation Mark gives: "For they had said, 'He has an unclean spirit' " (3:30). By means of this explanation, Mark stresses the opposition between an "unclean spirit" and God's "holy spirit." As Psalm 51 attests, it was common Jewish belief that every human being naturally possesses God's holy spirit. Jesus is teaching that the opposite of this state, that is, possession by an "unclean spirit," is thus unnatural or pathological. The "blasphemy against the holy spirit" is the denial of the fact that possession of God's holy spirit is every person's natural state. There is therefore no clearcut division, such as the scribes have implied, between good and evil persons; there are only people in varying states of pathology or wellness.

So Jesus, by driving out the unclean spirits, can restore people to their original wholeness. Sinners are invaded and bound by Satan; Jesus sets them free.

In Mark 3:22, **Beelzebul**, who is identified as "the prince of demons," is used as another name for Satan. The word "Beelzebul" is ultimately derived from the name of the Canaanite god Baal. In 2 Kings 1:2-3, 6, and 16, there is a pagan deity who is referred to by a similar name (the Hebrew *Baalzebub*). The meaning of this name can most readily be rendered "lord of the flies," clearly a scornful corruption of the pagan god's name.

3:31-35 Jesus' "brother and sister and mother"

In the final section of chapter 3, Mark shows Jesus redefining the meaning of family. Mark first shows the crowd around Jesus using the conventional meaning of "family" as those who are related in blood. Mark sets up this usual understanding so that he can present Jesus' unconventional teaching that "whoever does the will of God" is his "brother and sister and mother." This statement does not, of course, denigrate his blood relatives but simply elevates the essential quality of their kinship with him.

Mark initiates here what will become a growing theme in his Gospel, namely, that people cannot be labeled according to prefixed assumptions; they can only be defined by what they do. So no one can presume who constitutes a member of Jesus' family according to some external criterion. Jesus' brothers and sisters are simply those who act like him in relation to God and others. Later in his Gospel, Mark will show that this existential relationship with Jesus also applies to discipleship.

Jesus and His Family

31 His mother and his brothers arrived. Standing outside they sent word to him and called him.
32 A crowd seated around him told him, "Your mother and your brothers [and your sisters] are outside asking for you." 33 But he said to them in reply, "Who are my mother and [my] brothers?"
34 And looking around at those seated in the circle he said, "Here are my mother and my brothers.
35 [For] whoever does the will of God is my brother and sister and mother."

Summary of chapter 3

In chapter 3, Mark shows how Jesus challenges conventional ways of wisdom. Instead of shunning the man who is alienated from the religious community by his physical disability, Jesus summons him to the midst of the synagogue. In curing the man, he not only restores him but restores the Sabbath to its original purpose of celebrating God's creation of human life. Instead of fighting with unclean spirits and demanding their subservience to his powers, Jesus treats them as a human pathology, and once having cast them out of a person, he asks for their silence. For his disciples, he calls together a mixed lot of people, including his future betrayer. He seeks out closeness with people to the point where his family or his disciples consider him "out of his mind." He asserts that all sins will be forgiven except the sin of thinking that the holy spirit is not the natural possession of every human being. He finds his family not in blood bonds but in spiritual kinship. In all these ways, Mark shows Jesus to be at once the restorer of human wholeness and the challenger of conventional wisdom.

EXPLORING LESSON TWO

1. The four men who brought the paralytic to Jesus for healing were so determined that they went through the roof of the house (2:2-4). Describe a time or situation when friends or family have helped bring you or a loved one to Jesus.

2. a) The Greek terms Mark employs for Jesus' healing/forgiving of sickness/sin imply that Jesus is releasing them from being bound (see commentary on 2:5-7). When have you experienced forgiveness or healing as a form of release?

   b) Where in your community do you see the greatest need for the spiritual work of freeing or releasing those who are bound?

3. Jesus saw an opportunity to include and transform someone despised by others when he called Levi to follow him (2:13-17). What similar stories illustrate God's ability to work through "unacceptable" people? (See Luke 10:29-37; 19:1-10; John 4:4-26, 39-42.)

4. What does Jesus say or do in Mark 2:15-22 that reveals him to be a wisdom teacher? (To reflect on wisdom, see Prov 8:4-10; Sir 24:19-22; 51:23-26.)

5. What roles do fasting and feasting play in your own spiritual life (2:18-22)? What would you consider to be the ideal balance between them?

6. What does Jesus say and do that leads the Pharisees and Herodians to conspire to put him to death (2:23–3:6)?

7. What are some possible reasons Jesus did not want the demons to make his identity known (3:10-12)? (See Mark 1:32-34; Luke 4:40-41.)

8. a) Why has Jesus' family come to get him (3:21)?

   b) What qualifies a person as a member of Jesus' family (3:31-35)?

9. Did you learn anything new about Jesus in this section of Mark's Gospel? Did anything surprise you?

CLOSING PRAYER

He went up the mountain and summoned those whom he wanted and they came to him. (Mark 3:13)

Jesus, count us among those you call. Give us the desire to come to you and the energy needed to climb mountains. We pray this day for your followers who are in need of renewed energy and zeal, especially . . .

LESSON THREE

Mark 4–5

Begin your personal study and group discussion with a simple and sincere prayer such as:

Prayer

Loving God, open my mind and heart to hear your voice. Increase my understanding and inspire in me a greater desire to follow Jesus.

Read the Bible text of Mark 4–5 found in the outside columns of pages 44–53, highlighting what stands out to you.

Read the accompanying commentary to add to your understanding.

Respond to the questions on pages 55–56, Exploring Lesson Three.

The Closing Prayer on page 57 is for your personal use and may be used at the end of group discussion.

CHAPTER 4

The Parable of the Sower

[1]On another occasion he began to teach by the
sea. A very large crowd gathered around him so
that he got into a boat on the sea and sat down.
And the whole crowd was beside the sea on land.
[2]And he taught them at length in parables, and in
the course of his instruction he said to them,
[3]"Hear this! A sower went out to sow. [4]And as he
sowed, some seed fell on the path, and the birds
came and ate it up. [5]Other seed fell on rocky
ground where it had little soil. It sprang up at once
because the soil was not deep. [6]And when the sun
rose, it was scorched and it withered for lack of
roots. [7]Some seed fell among thorns, and the
thorns grew up and choked it and it produced no
grain. [8]And some seed fell on rich soil and pro-
duced fruit. It came up and grew and yielded
thirty, sixty, and a hundredfold." [9]He added,
"Whoever has ears to hear ought to hear."

continue

JESUS AS WISDOM TEACHER

Mark 4:1-41

4:1-34 The three seed parables

Parables are common to the style of the Wisdom writings, so it is in keeping with Mark's presentation of Jesus that he shows him teaching by means of them. It helps to know that in Jewish tradition a "parable" was a set form with a set purpose, not just an illustrative story. Most often it was a succinct way of suggesting what God, or God's kingdom, is like. And very often it formed this comparison by weaving together small pieces or echoes of Scripture. The suggestive analogy that emerged was one that interpreted the Bible passages at the same time that it used them to point to God's kingdom. The rabbis described parables as "making handles for the Torah," meaning that parables were intended to open up the meaning of the Bible—to help people "get a handle" on it.

Because parables were generally considered interpretations of the Bible, it was common practice for Jewish teachers to place several parables on the same theme next to each other so that the student could reflect on different possibilities of meaning. It was said that they placed them together "like pearls on a string." So when we see three parables on seeds placed together, we should assume that they are intended to be read in relationship to one another. This interrelated reading becomes even more urgent in view of Mark's habit of expressing himself in triads.

4:3-9 The parable of the sower

This parable is based on the common biblical image of God as a farmer sowing his seed. For example, in Isaiah 55:10-11, God says:

Yet just as from the heavens
  the rain and snow come down
And do not return there
  till they have watered the earth,
  making it fertile and fruitful,
Giving seed to the one who sows
  and bread to the one who eats,
So shall my word be
  that goes forth from my mouth;
It shall not return to me empty,
  but shall do what pleases me,
  achieving the end for which I sent it.

And underlying the poetic description of Genesis 1 is a similar image of God creating the whole universe by his word alone. God has only to say "Let there be light" and "there was light" (Gen 1:3). In these passages, God is a sower and his word is the fertile seed that creates the world.

In the parable that Mark shows Jesus telling first, the sower's seed is only partially successful. Unlike God's word in either Genesis or Isaiah, the seed does not entirely "achieve the end" for which God sends it. It is thwarted by birds (4:4), by "rocky ground" (4:5), and by "thorns" (4:7). Only when it falls on "rich soil" does it produce fruit (4:8). This divided result is at odds with the purpose of the Creator in Isaiah and in Genesis.

The vocabulary used to describe these results, moreover, intensifies the division. The birds *consumed* the seed (4:4); the sun "scorched" it, so that it "withered" (4:6); the thorns "choked" it (4:7). On the other hand, the seed that falls on good soil yields a superabundant harvest—"thirty, sixty, and a hundredfold" (4:8). The clearcut and exaggerated difference in results suggests an apocalyptic scenario—that is, a frightening view of the end time in which all people are revealed to have been predetermined to either eternal damnation or eternal bliss. Is that the teaching of Jesus here? We need to suspend our judgment until we have read the other two seed parables.

A **parable** is a short narrative that provides a descriptive metaphor or analogy for the "kingdom of God" or imparts a moral perspective. Only Matthew and Mark have parable chapters, large collections of Jesus' parables joined into one long discourse (Matt 13; Mark 4). Scholars agree that Jesus used parables as a special teaching technique, but parables would typically have been spoken as individual sayings given at different times and in different settings.

The Purpose of the Parables

10And when he was alone, those present along
with the Twelve questioned him about the parables.
11He answered them, "The mystery of the kingdom
of God has been granted to you. But to those out-
side everything comes in parables, 12so that

'they may look and see but not perceive,
and hear and listen but not understand,
in order that they may not be converted and
be forgiven.'"

13Jesus said to them, "Do you not understand this
parable? Then how will you understand any of the
parables? 14The sower sows the word. 15These are
the ones on the path where the word is sown. As
soon as they hear, Satan comes at once and takes
away the word sown in them. 16And these are the
ones sown on rocky ground who, when they hear
the word, receive it at once with joy. 17But they
have no root; they last only for a time. Then when
tribulation or persecution comes because of the
word, they quickly fall away. 18Those sown among
thorns are another sort. They are the people who
hear the word, 19but worldly anxiety, the lure of
riches, and the craving for other things intrude
and choke the word, and it bears no fruit. 20But
those sown on rich soil are the ones who hear the
word and accept it and bear fruit thirty and sixty
and a hundredfold."

Parable of the Lamp

21He said to them, "Is a lamp brought in to be
placed under a bushel basket or under a bed, and
not to be placed on a lampstand? 22For there is
nothing hidden except to be made visible; noth-
ing is secret except to come to light. 23Anyone
who has ears to hear ought to hear." 24He also told
them, "Take care what you hear. The measure with
which you measure will be measured out to you,
and still more will be given to you. 25To the one
who has, more will be given; from the one who
has not, even what he has will be taken away."

continue

Seed Grows of Itself

26He said, "This is how it is with the kingdom of God; it is as if a man were to scatter seed on the land 27and would sleep and rise night and day and the seed would sprout and grow, he knows not how. 28Of its own accord the land yields fruit, first the blade, then the ear, then the full grain in the ear. 29And when the grain is ripe, he wields the sickle at once, for the harvest has come."

The Mustard Seed

30He said, "To what shall we compare the kingdom of God, or what parable can we use for it? 31It is like a mustard seed that, when it is sown in the ground, is the smallest of all the seeds on the earth. 32But once it is sown, it springs up and becomes the largest of plants and puts forth large branches, so that the birds of the sky can dwell in its shade." 33With many such parables he spoke the word to them as they were able to understand

continue

4:26-29 The parable of the seed that grows by itself

This parable is unique to Mark's Gospel. If we read it in connection with the first seed parable, we find that it offers a picture so opposite that it is comic. In this scenario, the seed is so fertile it sprouts no matter what. Even while the farmer sleeps, the seed goes on growing, "he knows not how" (4:27). The words suggest something that has its own rhythm—"night and day" (4:27)—and cannot be stopped. Indeed, the phrase rendered here as "of its own accord" is literally in Greek "automatically"* (4:28). On automatic, the seed grows larger and larger until "the harvest has come" (4:29).

The first parable would make us wary and worried about our final destiny. This second parable reassures us that all shall be well. This kind of uncalculating trust in God suggests the wisdom that "the Preacher" arrives at in Ecclesiastes, when he says:

> One who pays heed to the wind will never sow,
> and one who watches the clouds will never reap.
> Just as you do not know how the life breath enters the human frame in the mother's womb,
> So you do not know the work of God,
> who is working in everything.
> In the morning sow your seed,
> and at evening do not let your hand be idle:
> For you do not know which of the two will be successful,
> or whether both alike will turn out well
> (Eccl 11:4-6).

The first parable presents the scary, apocalyptic view of an end time in which souls are predetermined to eternal bliss or damnation. The second presents the reassuring perspective of Wisdom that in spite of our limited ways, God is making all things work together for good.

This perspective is further emphasized by the fact that the line about wielding the sickle to cut the ripe harvest (4:29) actually echoes a passage in the prophet Joel where the harvest is sin and the sickle represents God's vengeance (4:13). Joel is giving the harvest imagery an abnormal, almost perverse meaning. Mark is reversing this reversal and turning the harvest imagery back into something positive and good.

As the middle parable, this second one is the key to the meaning of the triad. To understand the fullness of what Mark is presenting here as the teaching of Jesus, we need to look at the last one.

4:30-32 The parable of the mustard seed

The mustard seed as "the smallest of all the seeds" was proverbial in Palestine. What grows from it, however, while large for a plant (about eight feet), is not very tall in comparison with a tree. So the oft-repeated interpretation of this parable, that it is about a tiny seed growing into a huge tree, is misleadingly simplistic. Jews in Mark's audience would have been struck by several other aspects of this parable. First, they would have been surprised that anyone would have bothered to plant the mustard seed at all because it was so common. Mustard seed bushes grow all around the Lake of Galilee. Second, in the description of branches large enough to give shade to "the birds of the sky," they would have heard a direct echo of passages in Ezekiel and Daniel.

This echo, in fact, would have given them the real clue to the parable's meaning. In Ezekiel, God plants "a majestic cedar" so grand that "all kinds of winged birds will dwell / in the shade of its branches" (Ezek 17:22-23). In context, this grand tree is clearly a symbol of the Davidic kingdom. In the Book of Daniel, King Nebuchadnezzar asks Daniel to interpret a dream that includes this description of a tree:

> I saw a tree of great height at the center of the earth. It was large and strong, with its top touching the heavens, and it could be seen to the ends of the earth. Its leaves were beautiful, its fruit abundant, providing food for all. Under it the wild beasts found shade, in its branches the birds of the air nested; all flesh ate of it (Dan 4:7b-9).

The tree echoes the forbidden tree of Genesis 2, while its heaven-reaching top and nourishing of all flesh suggest "the tree of life" sealed off in the Garden.

By means of these echoes of Ezekiel and Daniel, the parable connects the common mustard seed plant with David's kingdom and with the tree of life in the first Garden. The real surprise in the parable is not the shift from small to large, but the paradoxical joining of the common and the ordinary with the divinely appointed grandeur of David and the divinely created nourishment of the original Garden. Through this imagery from the Bible, the parable suggests that the kingdom of God is analogous to something very common transformed into something grand and divinely life-giving.

Summary of the three parables

If we now read the three parables as a connected unit, we can see how they form a conversation about God's kingdom. The first parable presents a view of God's kingdom that was typical of apocalyptic writing of the time—that is, it suggests that God has created many people in this world but not all of them will be saved or arrive at God's kingdom. Some are destined to be lost. The labored allegorical explanation that is given in 4:14-20 may or may not be Mark's; many scholars think that it was added later. But whether it was or not, the parable itself invites that kind of exposition; it makes salvation the responsibility of the individual soul (or soil). The soil (or soul), moreover, appears predestined. There is no suggestion that the soil could change or that God's grace might intervene.

The second and third parables, however, present an entirely different point of view. The second parable, in fact, as we have seen, functions as a direct, almost comic refutation of the first, suggesting that no matter what, God's seed will grow and God's harvest will come. Its insistence on the unstoppable dynamism of God's seed prepares the way for the third parable, in which God's kingdom grows surprisingly out of common and ordinary seed.

It is worth noting that only the second and third parables are compared to God's kingdom (4:26, 30). As Mark presents Jesus' teaching, he does not introduce the first parable the same way. If we assume that all three parables must be read as a connected whole, then it appears that Jesus is not affirming the apocalyptic view here, but is going to some lengths to refute it. He is doing this in a way that is not familiar to us but would have been to a Jewish audience. He strings together three parables about seeds so his listeners will know they are interconnected. In the first, he gives the view that many of his day believed; in the next two, however, he undermines that view and offers some refuting wisdom. Through the second parable, he reminds his listeners of the wisdom of not trying to control everything, but to let go and trust in God's providence. Through the third parable, he reminds them that God created every human being (not just a few special ones) for the fullness of life.

4:10-13, 21-25 The purpose of the parables

In two different places in the chapter, Mark shows Jesus talking about his reason for teaching in parables. His first response seems almost perverse. He seems to be saying that he teaches in parables because he does not want everyone to understand him. But what he is actually doing is quoting Isaiah, and to understand his meaning, we have to know the context there.

The quotation comes from what is called Isaiah's "call story"—that is, it comes from the place in Isaiah where he recalls how he was first called by God to be a prophet. Every prophet has a similar story, and the stories follow a similar pattern. The prophet is always taken by surprise or put off balance by God's call. He accordingly always resists. Then God acts in some powerful way that makes the prophet realize that he has no choice. In Isaiah's case, he is first given a vision of God seated on a throne, worshiped by seraphim, who cry out, "Holy, holy, holy" while "the frame of the door shook and the house was filled with smoke" (Isa 6:3-4). Isaiah's first response is fear: "Then I said, 'Woe is me, I am doomed! For I am a man of unclean lips, living among a people of unclean lips, and my eyes have seen the King, the LORD of hosts!'" (Isa 6:5). God then sends one of the seraphim to him with an ember to purge his unclean lips. After that, God asks, "Whom shall I send?" and Isaiah answers, "Here I am . . . . send me!" (Isa 6:6-8). At that point, God tells him to "Go and say to this people":

> Listen carefully, but do not understand!
> Look intently, but do not perceive!
> Make the heart of this people sluggish,
> dull their ears and close their eyes;
> Lest they see with their eyes, and hear with their ears,
> and their heart understand,
> and they turn and be healed (Isa 6:9-10).

In context, God's words are clearly ironic. He is sending the prophet to the people because he wants them to "turn and be healed"; his saying the opposite only underscores how much he wants it. So when Mark shows Jesus quoting that passage here, we should also understand it as irony. Jesus' quotation of Isaiah links him to the prophet's mission and indicates that he, like Isaiah, is speaking so as to touch and heal hearts. He teaches in parables for that purpose.

Mark makes Jesus' intentions clearer a bit later when he has him compare his teaching to a lamp (4:21-25). In the Bible, a "lamp" is frequently used as a metaphor for God's word. The psalmist sings, "Your word is a lamp for my feet" (Ps 119:105), and the author of Proverbs says about one of the commandments, "For the command is a lamp, and the teaching a light" (Prov 6:23). So here, when Jesus asks if anyone would put a lamp under a bushel basket or a bed, he is suggesting that no one would try to hide God's word. Further, he is indicating that he certainly is not doing so. By implication, he is suggesting that the parable is a "lampstand" that will show off the light of God's word. The rabbis also speak of the parable form as a kind of lamp by which one can read the Bible more clearly.

When Jesus then goes on to say that "there is nothing hidden except to be made visible" and "nothing is secret except to come to light" (4:22), he appears to be expressing the Jewish view that the Bible contains God's revelation and nothing is hidden in the Bible except to be made clear.

The two proverbial sayings that follow—"The measure with which you measure will be measured out to you" (4:24) and "To the one who has, more will be given; from the one who has not, even what he has will be taken away" (4:25)—have a parallel in the Talmud, the most significant collection of the Jewish oral tradition. In the Talmud, it is clear that what is being talked about is the measure of one's understanding of God's word.

4:34-41 Jesus himself as parable

The parable section of the chapter appears to close with Mark telling us that "Without parables he [Jesus] did not speak to them [the crowd], but to his own disciples he explained everything in private" (4:34). The implication of this seems to be that Jesus did not use parables in teaching his disciples. It appears to confirm the earlier statement that Mark quotes Jesus as saying to his disciples: "The mystery of the kingdom of God has been granted to you. But to those outside everything comes in parables" (4:11). Yet the assertion is puzzling, because so far in his Gospel, Mark has not shown us Jesus teaching any other way.

What kind of distinction is Mark trying to make between Jesus' teaching of the crowd and his teaching of his disciples? In what special way has "the mystery of the kingdom of God" been granted to Jesus' disciples? In the closing verses of chapter 4, Mark seems to provide an answer. He shows Jesus himself to be a living parable. That is to say, in the final episode of Jesus' stilling the sea, Mark reveals that the person of Jesus provides an analogy to what God is like.

As in the parables that Jesus tells, this parable that he enacts is composed of echoes of Scripture. In this case, the direct echo is of some of the psalms that reflect on God's power over creation:

> Lord, God of hosts, who is like you? . . .
> You rule the raging sea;
> you still its swelling waves (Ps 89:9a, 10).
>
> You still the roaring of the seas,
> the roaring of their waves (Ps 65:8).
>
> [The Lord] hushed the storm to silence,
> the waves of the sea were stilled (Ps 107:29).

Mark, steeped in the Hebrew Bible himself, surely assumed that when he quotes the disciples saying, "Who then is this whom even wind and sea obey?" (4:41), his audience would have heard the answer in their memory of these psalms.

In the first part of chapter 4, Mark shows Jesus teaching in the style of a teacher of Wisdom, teaching in parables. At the end, however, he shows Jesus teaching by his actions. He shows Jesus stilling the sea as God stills the sea in the psalms. He shows Jesus to be "like God." He shows Jesus to be in himself a Wisdom parable. Those who are his disciples have been granted a direct encounter with "the mystery of the kingdom of God."

it. 34Without parables he did not speak to them, but to his own disciples he explained everything in private.

The Calming of a Storm at Sea

35On that day, as evening drew on, he said to them, "Let us cross to the other side." 36Leaving the crowd, they took him with them in the boat just as he was. And other boats were with him.
37A violent squall came up and waves were breaking over the boat, so that it was already filling up.
38Jesus was in the stern, asleep on a cushion. They woke him and said to him, "Teacher, do you not care that we are perishing?" 39He woke up, rebuked the wind, and said to the sea, "Quiet! Be still!" The wind ceased and there was great calm.
40Then he asked them, "Why are you terrified? Do you not yet have faith?" 41They were filled with great awe and said to one another, "Who then is this whom even wind and sea obey?"

continue

Summary of chapter 4

In chapter 4, Mark focuses on Jesus' teaching about the kingdom of God. He shows him teaching in the style of a Wisdom teacher, using parables to shed light on God's revelation in Scripture. He does so by following a method common to other Jewish teachers. He strings together three parables linked by the image of seeds. They are all based on the biblical image that expresses God the Creator as God the sower. Yet each one imagines God's sowing and the results differently. The first parable imagines God sowing some seeds that will bear fruit and some that will not. The second parable imagines God's word as a seed that will come to fruition no matter what. The third parable imagines God's word as a seed that is common and accessible, yet grows to be shade and shelter for all creatures.

In between the parables, Mark shows Jesus commenting on the purpose of parables. He first quotes the passage in Isaiah where God (by

CHAPTER 5

The Healing of the Gerasene Demoniac

1They came to the other side of the sea, to the
territory of the Gerasenes. 2When he got out of
the boat, at once a man from the tombs who had
an unclean spirit met him. 3The man had been
dwelling among the tombs, and no one could re-
strain him any longer, even with a chain. 4In fact,
he had frequently been bound with shackles and
chains, but the chains had been pulled apart by
him and the shackles smashed, and no one was
strong enough to subdue him. 5Night and day
among the tombs and on the hillsides he was al-
ways crying out and bruising himself with stones.
6Catching sight of Jesus from a distance, he ran
up and prostrated himself before him, 7crying out
in a loud voice, "What have you to do with me,
Jesus, Son of the Most High God? I adjure you
by God, do not torment me!" 8(He had been say-
ing to him, "Unclean spirit, come out of the
man!") 9He asked him, "What is your name?" He
replied, "Legion is my name. There are many of
us." 10And he pleaded earnestly with him not to
drive them away from that territory.

11Now a large herd of swine was feeding there
on the hillside. 12And they pleaded with him,
"Send us into the swine. Let us enter them." 13And
he let them, and the unclean spirits came out and
entered the swine. The herd of about two thou-
sand rushed down a steep bank into the sea, where
they were drowned. 14The swineherds ran away
and reported the incident in the town and
throughout the countryside. And people came
out to see what had happened. 15As they ap-
proached Jesus, they caught sight of the man who
had been possessed by Legion, sitting there
clothed and in his right mind. And they were
seized with fear. 16Those who witnessed the inci-
dent explained to them what had happened to the
possessed man and to the swine. 17Then they
began to beg him to leave their district. 18As he
was getting into the boat, the man who had been
possessed pleaded to remain with him. 19But he

continue

ironically saying the opposite of what he means) indicates how much he wants his word to touch and heal the human heart. He next suggests that the parable form is like a lampstand that shows off the light of God's word. He indicates that he speaks in parables in order to bring to light what is hidden in God's revelation.

Mark shows Jesus asking the question of how to find an analogy for God's kingdom. The second and third parables form one kind of answer. But in the final episode of the chapter, when Mark shows Jesus stilling the sea, he provides a different kind of answer. He shows Jesus himself acting the way God does in the psalms. He suggests that Jesus himself is a kind of parable, a living likeness of God. As a parable, he is like a lampstand that makes more visible the light of God's word. He is a living metaphor that serves to bring to light what is hidden in God's revelation.

THE TRANSFORMING EFFECT OF JESUS/WISDOM

Mark 5:1-43

5:1-20 The transformation of the Gerasene demoniac

No one knows exactly what Mark had in mind by "the territory of the Gerasenes," but it was clearly pagan territory, being on "the other side of the sea" from Galilee and inhabited by people who tended pigs (an unclean and forbidden animal to Jews). There are fascinating echoes of Isaiah's description of a pagan people who, he says, were "[s]itting in tombs," "[e]ating the flesh of pigs," and "[c]rying out, 'Hold back, / do not come near me!'" (Isa 65:4-5a). So we find here in Mark's narrative a man "dwelling among the tombs" whom "no one could restrain" (5:3), and who was "always crying out" (5:5). He is not said to be "eating swine's flesh," but swine do figure prominently in the story. In Isaiah, these pagan practices enkindle God's wrath (Isa 65:5b). Here, however, Mark shows Jesus treating them as evidence of unclean spirits, a pathological state that can be cured.

The narrative is also suggestive of Jesus' metaphor of "the strong man" in chapter 3. You may remember that there, Jesus observes, "No one can enter a strong man's house to plunder his property unless he first ties up the strong man" (3:27). Here in fact is a strong man, powerful enough to have pulled apart his physical chains (5:4), but nonetheless invaded and plundered by unclean spirits. Jesus' response is not to bind but to free him.

The exchange between Jesus and the unclean spirits reveals something about Mark's view of the nature of evil. First of all, like the unclean spirit in 1:24, the unclean spirits here cry out in protest at Jesus' appearance (5:7). Once again Mark indicates that they feel diminished by Jesus' very presence. Second, it should not be passed over that the name of these unclean spirits, "Legion," is the name of a unit in the Roman army. Surely a Jewish audience would have been amused by this piece of wit at their enemy's expense. Even more, they would have found it a joke that these Roman demons ask to be placed inside a herd of pigs. The final act in this rhetorical comedy is the scene of the pigs rushing headlong into the sea.

The serious side of this story is the pointed suggestion that those who were currently occupying Palestine and meddling with the Temple belong to the devil. At the time that Mark's Gospel was written down (probably the year 70), it would not have been safe or prudent for anyone to have said such a thing directly. But here and elsewhere, as we shall see, Mark insinuates his view of Rome.

After the unclean spirits leave him, the man who had been possessed reappears "clothed and in his right mind" (5:15). The details suggest that before, he had been naked and crazy; in ridding him of his demons, Jesus has restored him to himself. This restoration is such a profound change that it seems like a transformation. The ultimate sign of his transformation appears in the man's going off "to proclaim in Decapolis what Jesus had done for him" (5:20). Like the cured leper in 1:45, this man is transformed from an alienated human being into one who spreads the word of God's goodness.

would not permit him but told him instead, "Go home to your family and announce to them all that the Lord in his pity has done for you." [20]Then the man went off and began to proclaim in the Decapolis what Jesus had done for him; and all were amazed.

Jairus's Daughter and the Woman with a Hemorrhage

[21]When Jesus had crossed again [in the boat] to the other side, a large crowd gathered around him, and he stayed close to the sea. [22]One of the synagogue officials, named Jairus, came forward. Seeing him he fell at his feet [23]and pleaded earnestly with him, saying, "My daughter is at the point of death. Please, come lay your hands on her that she may get well and live." [24]He went off with him, and a large crowd followed him and pressed upon him.

continue

Gerasa (modern-day Jerash in Jordan) is situated thirty-three miles southeast of the Sea of Galilee. While both Mark and Luke (8:26) fix the site of this exorcism near Gerasa, Matthew relocates the scene to Gadara, a Hellenistic city much closer to the sea, thus making the conclusion of the narrative more plausible (Matt 8:28; note that in Luke's account, the swine rush into "the lake" rather than "the sea"). Some manuscripts have a third possible reading for the city/territory where this miracle occurred—Gergesa—which is based on speculation offered by the early church father Origen. Gergesa is most often identified with the modern-day city of Kursi, which is situated on the northeastern shore of the Sea of Galilee.

[25]There was a woman afflicted with hemorrhages for twelve years. [26]She had suffered greatly at the hands of many doctors and had spent all that she had. Yet she was not helped but only grew worse. [27]She had heard about Jesus and came up behind him in the crowd and touched his cloak. [28]She said, "If I but touch his clothes, I shall be cured." [29]Immediately her flow of blood dried up. She felt in her body that she was healed of her affliction. [30]Jesus, aware at once that power had gone out from him, turned around in the crowd and asked, "Who has touched my clothes?" [31]But his disciples said to him, "You see how the crowd is pressing upon you, and yet you ask, 'Who touched me?'" [32]And he looked around to see who had done it. [33]The woman, realizing what had happened to her, approached in fear and trembling. She fell down before Jesus and told him the whole truth. [34]He said to her, "Daughter, your faith has saved you. Go in peace and be cured of your affliction."

[35]While he was still speaking, people from the synagogue official's house arrived and said, "Your daughter has died; why trouble the teacher any longer?" [36]Disregarding the message that was reported, Jesus said to the synagogue official, "Do not be afraid; just have faith." [37]He did not allow anyone to accompany him inside except Peter, James, and John, the brother of James. [38]When they arrived at the house of the synagogue official, he caught sight of a commotion, people weeping and wailing loudly. [39]So he went in and said to them, "Why this commotion and weeping? The

continue

5:25-34 The transformation of the menstruating woman

The narrative of the woman who was suffering for twelve years from a menstrual disorder is interjected into the story of the twelve-year-old girl who appears to be dead. This structure of interlocking stories is a device Mark uses for a purpose. We will consider later what that purpose is.

The narrative of this woman is striking because in it Mark shows Jesus dealing openly and compassionately with a female condition that was taboo. Menstruating women were considered ritually unclean and excluded from Temple gatherings. Menstruating women were considered sexually unclean, so husbands were forbidden to have intercourse with them. In biblical writings, a menstruating woman is used as a symbol of idolatry. Thus, to describe a woman who had suffered from a flow of menstrual blood over a period of twelve years is to hold up for consideration a woman who in every way sums up "the unclean" within Judaism—ritually, sexually, and religiously. Her healing contact with Jesus thus has significance far beyond the immediate miracle. Mark suggests that she was changed in two different ways: first, "she felt in her body that she was healed of her affliction" (5:29), and second, she receives an affirmation of her faith (5:34).

There are details in the scene worth noting. First, Mark underlines the spiritual significance of the story by his repeated use of "straightway." He tells us that "*Straightway** her flow of blood dried up" (5:29) and *Straightway* Jesus was aware that "power had gone out from him" (5:30).

Second, Mark says that the woman approached Jesus "in fear and trembling" (5:33). The phrase anticipates the description of the three women before the empty tomb and should be kept in mind as a clue to its meaning. Clearly, the woman here is trembling because she has sensed the power that has healed her body; she is not frightened but in awe of it. When we read later that the women at the tomb were also "trembling" (16:8), we should remember that Mark has used the word here to signify the holy state of being overwhelmed by God's power. Mark confirms this meaning when he quotes Jesus as saying, "Daughter, your faith has saved you" (5:34a). Mark confirms this further by showing Jesus bestowing on her a traditional Jewish blessing: "Go [or walk] in peace . . . ." (5:34a). The woman has been transformed by Jesus from someone who was ostracized as "unclean" into a model of faith.

> child is not dead but asleep." 40 And they ridiculed him. Then he put them all out. He took along the child's father and mother and those who were with him and entered the room where the child was. 41 He took the child by the hand and said to her, "*Talitha koum*," which means, "Little girl, I say to you, arise!" 42 The girl, a child of twelve, arose immediately and walked around. [At that] they were utterly astounded. 43 He gave strict orders that no one should know this and said that she should be given something to eat.

Vestiges of **Aramaic** and **Hebrew** can be found in the New Testament, although the New Testament is written in Koine ("common") Greek, the language of the Roman Empire at the time of Jesus. Aramaic was the language spoken by Jews in daily life, while Hebrew was the formal language of the written Scriptures and liturgical services. In addition to place names (Gehenna, Golgotha, etc.) and the liturgical word *amen* ("so be it"), the main Aramaic-Hebrew expressions found in the New Testament include:

Talitha koum (Little girl, arise!)	Mark 5:41
Qorban (dedicated to God)	Mark 7:11
Ephphatha (Be opened!)	Mark 7:34
Abba (dearest father)	Mark 14:36; Rom 8:15; Gal 4:6
Raqa (evil)	Matt 5:22
Eloi, Eloi, lema sabachthani? (My God, my God, why have you forsaken me?)	Mark 15:34; Matt 27:46

5:21-24, 35-43 The transformation of the synagogue leader's daughter

After the story of Jesus' transformation of the possessed man in the pagan, Gentile world of the Gerasenes, Mark says that Jesus crossed the Sea of Galilee again, back to the Jewish side (5:21). Here Mark begins the story of Jairus, the synagogue official who begs for help for his dying daughter (5:22-24). Mark interrupts that narrative to tell the one of the menstruating woman, then returns to it after she has been healed and sent off in peace. The interruption serves two purposes: first, it provides a narrative reason for Jesus' delay in going to see the little girl, an interval that appears to be fatal (5:35), so that, dramatically, Jesus' miracle here has greater dimensions than a simple healing. Second, it makes the story of the older woman shed light on the meaning of the little girl's, and vice versa. Intertwined as narratives, they are also intertwined in meaning. In both cases, a female person is brought back from the brink of death.

Mark shapes the narrative of the little girl so as to show that this is a story of resurrection—one that anticipates Jesus' own. He quotes Jesus as saying three things in the course of the story, each of them pointing to the story's ultimate significance. Jesus says to the synagogue official, "Do not be afraid; just have faith" (5:36). He says to the weeping crowd, "The child is not dead but asleep" (5:39). And he says to the child herself, "Rise up!"* (5:41).

Each one of these comments is geared toward transforming common attitudes toward death. To the synagogue official, death was not only an occasion of sadness but of fear, because it was believed at the time that death rendered the human body "unclean" and so made anyone who touched it ritually unclean. To the crowd "weeping and wailing loudly" (5:38), death was final, and to the child herself, life seemed over. Against these views, Jesus' comments exchange fear for faith, suggest that death is but a temporary and reversible phase, and call the child back to life.

Once again, as in the healing of Simon's mother-in-law (1:31) and the healing of the paralytic (2:11), Mark uses the same word here for "rise" that he uses for Jesus' resurrection. Mark also uses key words to describe the reaction of the witnesses. What is translated here as "They were utterly astounded" (5:42b) is literally "They were out of their minds [or "beside themselves"] with ecstasy."* The phrase "out of their minds" echoes Mark's earlier description of those who witnessed the paralytic rise up (2:12b) and the place where those close to Jesus think he is "out of his mind" (3:21). Mark will use the word "ecstasy" again at the end of his Gospel to describe the experience of the women overwhelmed by God's power to overcome death.

In ancient Israel, belief in life after death was very limited, and the concept of the **resurrection of the body** was unknown. It was generally held that at the time of death, everyone—good and bad—went to a place called Sheol, sometimes translated "netherworld" or "underworld." Existence in Sheol was little better than suspended animation: there was no pain, no joy, no memory, no communication, no light. These religious views gradually began to change in the post-exilic period. In the Wisdom of Solomon (written possibly as late as the first century B.C.E.), for example, death is not depicted as a state of "utter destruction" (3:3) but as the gateway to a "hope full of immortality" (3:4). Belief in the resurrection of the body likewise gained momentum in the same period, as is evident in 2 Maccabees (7:9, 11, 14, 23; 12:44) and Daniel 12:2. In Jesus' time, belief in the resurrection of the body was championed by the Pharisees while it was opposed by the Sadducees, who found no warrant for the doctrine in the Pentateuch.

Summary of chapter 5

In this chapter, Mark shows Jesus having a transforming effect on different states considered "unclean" within Judaism: demonic possession, menstruation, and death. Considering these three episodes as another Markan triad, we need to explore how the middle episode is key. The first transforming miracle takes place in the Gentile world; the last is set in the home of a synagogue leader. The first frees a man from his demons and restores him to himself; the last raises up a child thought dead and restores her to her parents. In the middle is the transformation of a Jewish woman whose physical condition has alienated her as completely from the Temple and synagogue as demons or death. In curing her, Jesus restores her both to herself and to her religious community. In effect, he brings her back to life.

EXPLORING LESSON THREE

1. What experience do you have of planting seeds in a container, a garden, or on a farm? What insights into the growth of God's word does your experience give you (4:1-9)?

2. What obstacles to the growth of the seeds God plants have you encountered in yourself and/or in others? How do you deal with these obstacles (4:10-20)?

3. Jesus seems to say that he uses parables to purposely obscure his message and make it impossible for "those outside" to understand him (4:11-12). But in 4:22-23, he seems to say the opposite: "there is nothing hidden except to be made visible." How might these two passages be reconciled? (See Matt 13:13-15; Isa 6:9-10.)

4. Which of the four parables of seeds and light speaks most profoundly to you (4:1-34)? Why?

5. How does the scene of Jesus calming the waters demonstrate God's nature (4:35-41)? Recount a time when faith has helped you weather a storm in life.

6. What details of the Gerasene demoniac's living situation reveal how far he was outside of Jewish religious sensibilities (5:1-20)?

7. What do you find most remarkable or meaningful about the healing of the hemorrhaging woman (5:25-34)?

8. What restorations in relationships do each of the three healings in 5:1-43 bring about (the demoniac in 5:1-20; the woman with the hemorrhage in 5:25-34; and Jairus's daughter in 5:21-24; 5:35-43)?

CLOSING PRAYER

"Teacher, do you not care that we are perishing?" (Mark 4:38)

Jesus, show us that while our fears and anxieties may ride with us in life's boat, they will not have the power to capsize us. Only your power can fully calm the storms within and around us. Teach us to trust in you more deeply and to call upon you when we are in trouble. We pray now for those situations in our world that cause fear and anxiety, especially those we share now . . .

LESSON FOUR

Mark 6–7

Begin your personal study and group discussion with a simple and sincere prayer such as:

Prayer

Loving God, open my mind and heart to hear your voice. Increase my understanding and inspire in me a greater desire to follow Jesus.

Read the Bible text of Mark 6–7 found in the outside columns of pages 60–70, highlighting what stands out to you.

Read the accompanying commentary to add to your understanding.

Respond to the questions on pages 72–73, Exploring Lesson Four.

The Closing Prayer on page 74 is for your personal use and may be used at the end of group discussion.

CHAPTER 6

The Rejection at Nazareth

1He departed from there and came to his native place, accompanied by his disciples. 2When the sabbath came he began to teach in the synagogue, and many who heard him were astonished. They said, "Where did this man get all this? What kind of wisdom has been given him? What mighty deeds are wrought by his hands! 3Is he not the carpenter, the son of Mary, and the brother of James and Joses and Judas and Simon? And are not his sisters here with us?" And they took offense at him. 4Jesus said to them, "A prophet is not without honor except in his native place and among his own kin and in his own house." 5So he was not able to perform any mighty deed there, apart from curing a few sick people by laying his hands on them. 6He was amazed at their lack of faith.

The Mission of the Twelve

He went around to the villages in the vicinity teaching. 7He summoned the Twelve and began to send them out two by two and gave them authority over unclean spirits. 8He instructed them to take nothing for the journey but a walking stick—no food, no sack, no money in their belts. 9They were, however, to wear sandals but not a second tunic. 10He said to them, "Wherever you enter a house, stay there until you leave from there. 11Whatever place does not welcome you or listen to you, leave there and shake the dust off your feet in testimony against them." 12So they went off and preached repentance. 13They drove out many demons, and they anointed with oil many who were sick and cured them.

Herod's Opinion of Jesus

14King Herod heard about it, for his fame had become widespread, and people were saying, "John the Baptist has been raised from the dead; that is why mighty powers are at work in him." 15Others were saying, "He is Elijah"; still others, "He is a prophet like any of the prophets." 16But

continue

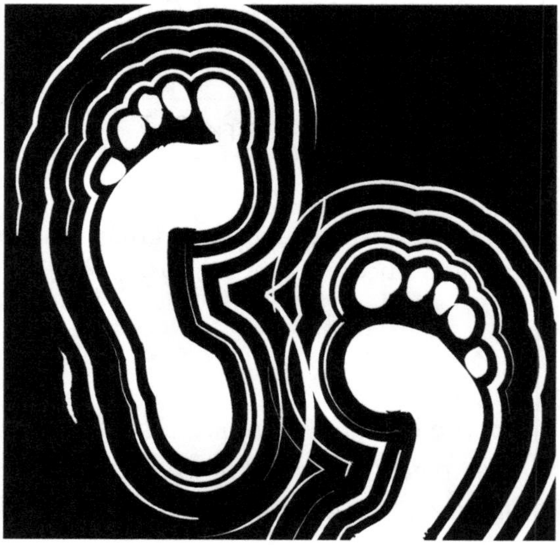

THE RECOGNITION OF JESUS/WISDOM

Mark 6:1-56

6:1-6 Jesus as too familiar

In the preceding chapters, Mark has repeatedly dramatized how people around Jesus are challenged by his unconventional ways. They are challenged by his "new teaching" (1:27) that possession by demons is a pathological state that can be cured (1:21-28; 3:22-30); by his transforming outreach to "the unclean" (1:40-45; 5:1-43); by his "raising up"* of women (1:29-31; 5:21-43); by his calling of sinners (2:13-17) and his views on sin and forgiveness (3:22-30); by his seeming indifference to religious rules (2:18-28); by his priorities—by the way he continually places human need first (3:1-5); by his redefining the meaning of "family" (3:31-35); by his teaching in parables (4:1-34); by his easy command of demons and storms (1:25; 4:39; 5:8).

At the beginning of chapter 6, Mark dramatizes the opposite: he constructs a scene in which the people in Jesus' hometown find him too familiar to teach them anything. The questions that Mark quotes them as asking are typical of all people who expect (or want) their encounter with the divine to be unusual and spectacular.

Since Mark has been presenting Jesus to his readers as Wisdom herself, there is particular irony in their question "What kind of wisdom has been given him?" (6:2). With further irony, Mark uses their questions to set up Jesus' Wisdom-saying, "A prophet is not without honor except in his native place and among his own kin and in his own house" (6:4). In this pithy observation, Mark shows Jesus also hinting at the destiny of his disciples.

6:7-13, 30-31 The commissioning of the disciples of Jesus/Wisdom

Mark shows that the disciples are instructed to imitate Jesus in preaching repentance, driving out demons, and curing the sick (6:12-13). By implication, the instruction to be detached from their possessions (6:8-9) also reflects the simple lifestyle of Jesus/Wisdom, a point Mark will develop in chapter 10. Mark links this narrative to the scene in Nazareth by showing that Jesus tells them to expect rejection (6:11). Later in the chapter, Mark shows how the disciples return to report and how Jesus invites them to follow him further by withdrawing for prayer (6:30-31).

6:14-29 The death of John the Baptist

As in chapter 5, Mark interweaves different narratives, so that each one comments on the other. As we have seen, one narrative strand is concerned with the disciples—how they are sent forth to be like Jesus and how they return to report. In between we hear the story of John the Baptist. Although at first hearing the transition may seem abrupt and the stories unconnected, with hindsight we can see that Mark has set up the narrative about John and his followers to foreshadow the narrative of Jesus and his disciples. Mark builds upon the original connections he has made between John and Jesus (1:14; 2:18) to achieve this effect.

Mark uses the device of a conversation about Jesus and John to set up the connections. First we hear people in general comparing Jesus with John (6:14), and then we hear Herod making the same comparison (6:16). In both instances, these voices speak of John as "raised from the dead." It is only then, and in retrospect, that we hear how and why John was murdered by Herod.

The story is complex, dramatizing the convergence of many causes. The root cause is

---

when Herod learned of it, he said, "It is John whom I beheaded. He has been raised up."

The Death of John the Baptist

[17]Herod was the one who had John arrested and bound in prison on account of Herodias, the wife of his brother Philip, whom he had married. [18]John had said to Herod, "It is not lawful for you to have your brother's wife." [19]Herodias harbored a grudge against him and wanted to kill him but was unable to do so. [20]Herod feared John, knowing him to be a righteous and holy man, and kept him in custody. When he heard him speak he was very much perplexed, yet he liked to listen to him. [21]She had an opportunity one day when Herod, on his birthday, gave a banquet for his courtiers, his military officers, and the leading men of Galilee. [22]Herodias's own daughter came in and performed a dance that delighted Herod and his guests. The king said to the girl, "Ask of me whatever you wish and I will grant it to you." [23]He even swore [many things] to her, "I will grant you whatever you ask of me, even to half of my kingdom." [24]She went out and said to her mother, "What shall I ask for?" She replied, "The head of John the Baptist." [25]The girl hurried back to the king's presence and made her request, "I want you to give me at once on a platter the head of John the Baptist." [26]The king was deeply distressed, but because of his oaths and the guests he did not wish to break his word to her. [27]So he promptly dispatched an executioner with orders to bring back his head. He went off and beheaded him in the prison. [28]He brought in the head on a platter and gave it to the girl. The girl in turn gave it to her mother. [29]When his disciples heard about it, they came and took his body and laid it in a tomb.

continue

---

classic: a prophet (John) "speaks truth to power." Nonetheless, we are told, Herod himself would not have injured John on that account, because he "feared John" and "liked to listen to him" (6:20). His wife, Herodias, however, angered at being denounced as unlawful, "harbored a grudge" and looked for the chance to avenge herself (6:19). The opportunity presents itself in the form of Herod's birthday party, a seemingly innocuous celebration (6:21). There the dance of a young girl (the daughter of Herodias) leads to Herod's extravagant and thoughtless vow: "I will grant you whatever you ask of me, even to half of my kingdom" (6:23). The plot concludes in a dizzying series of ironies: the young girl acts like a dutiful and docile daughter in repeating to Herod her mother's murderous request for "the head of John the Baptist" (6:24). The king, although "deeply distressed," accedes to the request out of a sense of fidelity to his word (6:26). The girl, dutiful to the end, took the prophet's head and "gave it to her mother" (6:28).

Mark has told the story of John's death in a way that illuminates how it results from a tragic and ironic mixture of vengeful hatred, chance opportunity, filial devotion, and vacillating weakness. As Mark tells the story, it is clear that while there is certainly some real evil at work (the unlawful marriage to begin with, and then the desire for revenge on the part of Herodias), the murder would never have been accomplished without Herod's weak ambivalence. Even though he knew John "to be a righteous and holy man," he had him imprisoned (6:17, 20), and even though he was "deeply distressed" (6:26) by the girl's

Getting It Right . . . Which Herod? The New Testament features several kings from the same royal family whose names are Herod. Antipater I, grandfather of Herod the Great, was the founder of the Herodian dynasty (second century B.C.E.). They were Idumeans (from the region of Idumea) who converted to Judaism. After Herod the Great's death, the Roman emperor divided Herod's kingdom among his three sons. Throughout the New Testament period, the Herodian rulers relied extensively on the Roman emperors to reinforce their authority, a tactic that Herod the Great's father, Antipater II, had begun in the early first century B.C.E. The New Testament reference to certain "Herodians" likely refers to political supporters of Herod Antipas (Matt 22:16; Mark 3:6; 12:13).

Name	Description	Key NT References
Herod the Great	Ruled 37–4 B.C.E.; built the Temple in Jerusalem, called the second Temple	Matt 2:1-12
Archelaus (son)	Ruled 4 B.C.E.–6 C.E.; inherited Judea and Samaria as "king" from his father but was an ineffectual ruler removed rather quickly by Rome	Matt 2:22
Herod Antipas (son)	Ruled 4 B.C.E.–39 C.E. as tetrarch of Galilee; beheaded John the Baptist, who opposed the marriage to his brother Philip's wife Herodias	Matt 14:1; Mark 6:17; Luke 3:1, 19; 9:7; Acts 13:1
Philip the Tetrarch (son)	Ruled 4 B.C.E.–34 C.E.; Roman-educated and capable ruler; expanded Panias and renamed it Caesarea Philippi	Matt 14:3; Mark 6:17; Luke 3:1
Herod Agrippa I	Ruled 41–44 C.E.; beheaded James, son of John ca. 44 C.E.	Acts 12:1-23
Herod Agrippa II	Ruled 53–93 C.E.; supported Rome during the Jewish revolt 66–70 C.E.	Acts 25:13–26:32

savage request, he gave the order for John's beheading (6:27).

Mark's narrative and theological purpose in telling this story is revealed in the conclusion: "When his disciples heard about it, they came and took his body and laid it in a tomb" (6:29). Mark has put the story of John's death here as a foreshadowing of Jesus' death. The two stories are not, of course, exactly the same, but there are parallels. In the second part of his Gospel, Mark will show Jesus speaking some unwelcome truths to those in power, and he will suggest how some leaders (both Roman and Jewish) were resentful of this criticism, and so looked for a way to get rid of him. He will show the collaboration between these vengeful people and the opportunist Judas (14:10-11). But above all, he will show how it is Pilate's weakness, especially his desire "to satisfy the crowd," that results in his condemnation of Jesus (15:15).

Mark also uses this story to illuminate the difference between John's disciples and those of Jesus. Unlike John's disciples, Jesus' disciples do not come as a group to ask for his body and bury it. One person, Joseph of Arimathea, does come, but he is a member of the council that condemned Jesus and so a new and unexpected disciple. All the others have fled. It is with pointed irony that Mark makes this story of John and his faithful disciples part of the narrative in which Jesus' disciples receive their instructions.

Finally, Mark uses this story to foreshadow Jesus' resurrection. He does this through the opening speculation by the people and by Herod that Jesus may in fact be John "raised up." Before this, Mark has introduced the motif of resurrection through the vocabulary of "rising up" and "raised up" that he uses for so many of Jesus' miracles. Here Mark makes the resurrection theme explicit.

It is also worth noting that Mark sets up a structure here that he will repeat in connection with Jesus. He gives a hint of John's resurrection before he tells us about his death, just as he will tell of Jesus' transfiguration before he gives an account of his passion. In this way, too, Mark uses John's story to foreshadow that of Jesus.

The Return of the Twelve

30The apostles gathered together with Jesus and reported all they had done and taught. 31He said to them, "Come away by yourselves to a deserted place and rest a while." People were coming and going in great numbers, and they had no opportunity even to eat. 32So they went off in the boat by themselves to a deserted place. 33People saw them leaving and many came to know about it. They hastened there on foot from all the towns and arrived at the place before them.

The Feeding of the Five Thousand

34When he disembarked and saw the vast crowd, his heart was moved with pity for them, for they were like sheep without a shepherd; and he began to teach them many things. 35By now it was already late and his disciples approached him and said, "This is a deserted place and it is already very late. 36Dismiss them so that they can go to

continue

6:31-44 The feeding of the five thousand

The motif of food and of eating is a recurring one in Mark's Gospel. It causes criticism when Jesus is seen eating with sinners and tax collectors (2:16). It raises questions when Jesus and his disciples feast rather than fast (2:18-19). It occasions moral outrage when Jesus allows his disciples to pick grain on the Sabbath, and the outrage in turn provides the opportunity for Jesus to teach that God's intent for the Sabbath is human wholeness (2:23-28).

All this concern with nurture is part of Mark's portrayal of Jesus as Wisdom—a womanly figure in Proverbs (and elsewhere), who ceaselessly invites guests to the divine banquet. In keeping with these motherly characteristics, Mark shows Jesus' first concern for Jairus's daughter, once he has brought her back to life, is that "she should be given something the surrounding farms and villages and buy themselves something to eat." [37]He said to them in reply, "Give them some food yourselves." But they said to him, "Are we to buy two hundred days' wages worth of food and give it to them to eat?" [38]He asked them, "How many loaves do you have? Go and see." And when they had found out they said, "Five loaves and two fish." [39]So he gave orders to have them sit down in groups on the green grass. [40]The people took their places in rows by hundreds and by fifties. [41]Then, taking the five loaves and the two fish and looking up to heaven, he said the blessing, broke the loaves, and gave them to [his] disciples to set before the people; he also divided the two fish among them all. [42]They all ate and were satisfied. [43]And they picked up twelve wicker baskets full of fragments and what was left of the fish. [44]Those who ate [of the loaves] were five thousand men.

continue

to eat" (5:43). That verse, which is the conclusion of chapter 5, prepares for Jesus' concern here for feeding the five thousand who have followed him.

Mark constructs a transition from the narrative of Jesus and the disciples to this narrative by noting that they were surrounded by so many people that "they had no opportunity even to eat" (6:31). There is an echo here of the earlier scene where "the crowds gathered, making it impossible for them even to eat" (3:20). In the earlier instance, Mark tells us that those close to Jesus said, "He is out of his mind" (3:21). In this instance, Mark says that Jesus and his disciples set off "to a deserted place" (6:32) but could not keep the crowds away. Mark then describes a repetition of what happened at the end of chapter 1 when Jesus "remained in deserted places," and yet "people kept coming to him from everywhere" (1:45b). Here again Mark dramatizes that Jesus cannot escape the crowds. They arrive at his destination on foot before he arrives at it by boat (6:32-33).

In the scenes that follow, Mark suggests in several different ways that Jesus is acting the way God acts in the Hebrew Bible. When Mark tells us that Jesus' heart was "moved with pity for them, for they were like sheep without a shepherd" (6:34), he is echoing the place in Ezekiel where God pities the hungry sheep and promises to shepherd them himself (Ezek 34:11-15).

When Mark tells us that Jesus ordered the people to "sit down in groups," the words literally are "meal-sharing groups"* (6:39). This phrasing is suggestive of God's instructions for sharing the Passover meal: "If a household is too small for a lamb, it along with its nearest neighbor will procure one," and shall share in the lamb (Exod 12:4).

Through the threefold repetition of "deserted place" (6:31a, 32, 35), Mark emphasizes that the setting is similar to the wilderness setting of the Exodus journey.

Mark thus tells the story of Jesus' miraculous feeding of the five thousand in the desert in such a way that it would remind his audience of God's miraculous way of providing his people with manna in the desert. In this context, Jesus' invitation to come to the desert ("Come away . . . and rest a while," 6:31a) is suggestive of God's command not even to gather manna on the seventh day but to share his Sabbath rest (Exod 16:23).

The overall thrust of the book of Exodus is God's providential care for his people, not only in leading them out of slavery but in leading them into a space and time apart from ordinary concerns—into a desert place and Sabbath time where they could learn to become dependent on God for food and life itself. By echoing this crucial time in the history of God's people, Mark suggests how Jesus reflects this nurturing aspect of God.

6:45-52 Walking on water

In describing Jesus' "walking on the sea" (6:48b), Mark shows Jesus acting like God in Job (9:8 and 38:16) and Sirach (24:5-6). Other miraculous actions of Jesus have some precedent in one of the prophets: Elisha multiplies bread (2 Kgs 4:42-44) and cures the leper Naaman (2 Kgs 5:1-14); Elijah raises a young man from the dead (1 Kgs 17:17-24). But no prophet walks on water. In describing this scene, Mark is dramatizing his perception that Jesus resembles God himself. Mark intensifies this perception by showing Jesus still the waters once again as he did at the end of chapter 4. There we noted that Mark, through echoes of Psalm 89, suggests that Jesus is a living parable of what God is like. When Mark repeats the scene here, he makes that likeness clear.

The reaction of the disciples, however, to this second incident of Jesus' stilling the sea is markedly less perceptive than the first time around. This time, when they see Jesus walking to them on the water, they are not awed but terrified. (Here Mark uses a verb that means "fright," not "holy fear.") When the wind dies down, they do not ask, as they did before, "Who then is this, whom even wind and sea obey?" (4:41). In the earlier incident, Mark suggests that they might be coming to a deeper understanding of Jesus' identity. In this scene, however, he says that "they had not understood the incident of the loaves. On the contrary, their hearts were hardened" (6:52).

"Hardness of heart," as we have noted before, is a typical way for the Hebrew Bible to express the obstinate resistance of the sinner to God's outreach. Mark has used it before in his Gospel to describe the Pharisees' cold reaction to Jesus' healing of the man with a withered hand (3:5). It is striking that he uses the same phrase here to describe the obtuse response of Jesus' own disciples.

6:53-56 Recognition of Jesus at Gennesaret

Mark concludes the chapter with a sharply contrasting description of the ordinary crowds. Most telling is the phrase "people straightway* recognized him" (6:54). It is striking because the chapter opens with Mark dramatizing a scene in Jesus' hometown in which people who "know" him cannot recognize him as anything more than "the carpenter, the son of Mary" (6:3).

The Walking on the Water

45 Then he made his disciples get into the boat and precede him to the other side toward Bethsaida, while he dismissed the crowd. 46 And when he had taken leave of them, he went off to the mountain to pray. 47 When it was evening, the boat was far out on the sea and he was alone on shore. 48 Then he saw that they were tossed about while rowing, for the wind was against them. About the fourth watch of the night, he came toward them walking on the sea. He meant to pass by them. 49 But when they saw him walking on the sea, they thought it was a ghost and cried out. 50 They had all seen him and were terrified. But at once he spoke with them, "Take courage, it is I, do not be afraid!" 51 He got into the boat with them and the wind died down. They were [completely] astounded. 52 They had not understood the incident of the loaves. On the contrary, their hearts were hardened.

The Healings at Gennesaret

53 After making the crossing, they came to land at Gennesaret and tied up there. 54 As they were leaving the boat, people immediately recognized

continue

The importance of the recognition here is underlined by Mark's use of the word "straightway." While Jesus' own disciples fail to understand anything significant in Jesus' feeding of the five thousand, the crowds scurry to bring their sick, and like the woman with the disordered flow of blood (5:28), they "begged him that they might touch only the tassel on his cloak" (6:56).

Summary of chapter 6

In this chapter, Mark dwells on the theme of people recognizing or not recognizing Jesus as God's Wisdom. In the opening scene, he shows people in Jesus' hometown not recognizing him as anyone special because he is so familiar. In the last scene of the chapter, Mark him. 55They scurried about the surrounding country and began to bring in the sick on mats to wherever they heard he was. 56Whatever villages or towns or countryside he entered, they laid the sick in the marketplaces and begged him that they might touch only the tassel on his cloak; and as many as touched it were healed.

CHAPTER 7

The Tradition of the Elders

1Now when the Pharisees with some scribes who had come from Jerusalem gathered around him, 2they observed that some of his disciples ate their meals with unclean, that is, unwashed, hands. 3(For the Pharisees and, in fact, all Jews, do not eat without carefully washing their hands, keeping the tradition of the elders. 4And on coming from the marketplace they do not eat without purifying themselves. And there are many other things that they have traditionally observed, the purification of cups and jugs and kettles [and beds].) 5So the Pharisees and scribes questioned him, "Why do your disciples not follow the tradi-

continue

shows ordinary crowds elsewhere recognizing him "straightway." These two extremes frame the chapter.

In between, Mark dwells on the role of the disciples and their variable responses to Jesus and to his actions. Again there is a framework of two extremes: early in the chapter we see the disciples sent forth to imitate Jesus in his preaching, healing, and exorcising of demons, yet at the end of the chapter we find that "their hearts were hardened," so that they remember neither Jesus' miracle of the loaves nor his earlier command of the sea.

The complicated, uncertain nature of the disciples is further dramatized through Mark's device of interweaving the story of John the Baptist into their story. The narrative of John's death and the possibility of his being "raised up" function as a foreshadowing of the death and resurrection of Jesus. At the same time, Mark sets up the courageous, faithful disciples of John as a contrast to the disciples of Jesus, who, in the end, will become frightened (as they are here) and run away.

And even while he is showing the disciples as repeatedly unable to grasp who Jesus is, Mark is dramatizing more and more clearly that Jesus is the image of God. Jesus feeds the crowds with bread in the desert as God fed the Israelites with manna in the wilderness; he walks on water as God does in Job and Sirach.

JESUS' REDEFINING OF THE "UNCLEAN"

Mark 7:1-37

7:1-13 Discussion of the sacred and the profane

In Jewish tradition, there are clear boundaries between the sacred and the profane, between what is to be consecrated to God and what is to be regarded as secular or "common." The Jewish people see themselves as consecrated to God in accordance with God's blessing of them in Exodus 19:6: "You will be to me a kingdom of priests, a holy nation." The Ten Commandments of the covenant, as well as the subsidiary laws designed to support and protect them, are considered a gift to be cherished.

The laws concerning food are part of this larger context. Eating kosher food and using kosher dishes are an acknowledgment that all life, as well as the nourishing of it, is sacred to the Lord. The whole discussion in this chapter should be regarded in that context and not as an argument over trivial rules. The Jewish custom of washing their hands before eating, and the vessels before using them, was originally more than good hygiene. They were also acts of ritual purification, signaling Jewish desire to consecrate this most basic of human activities.

Unfortunately, verses 3 and 4, which try to give an explanation for these washing rituals, are flawed in the original manuscript. Verse 3 literally reads, "For the Pharisees and all the

Jews do not eat unless they have washed themselves *with the fist** . . . ." Verse 4 literally reads, "And they do not eat from the marketplace unless they immerse themselves, and there are many other traditions they carry out, the immersing of cups and pots and bronze vessels *and beds.**" No translator knows what to do with "the fist" in verse 3 or the "beds" of verse 4. No commentator notes that the word "immerse" here is *baptizo* in Greek. It's a word that Mark uses for baptism but is ill-suited to this context. Many scholars think that this curious explanation of Jewish customs was probably added to Mark's manuscript after the first century. Vincent Taylor, one of the best of these scholars, recommends skipping verses 2-4 entirely.

In any case, Mark uses a favorite device here: he cites a question by the Pharisees in order to set up Jesus' teaching on what is and is not sacred. The Pharisees challenge the eating customs of Jesus' disciples, just as earlier they had challenged their picking grain on the Sabbath (2:24). The language of this challenge highlights what is at stake: "Why do your disciples . . . eat a meal with unclean hands?" (7:5). The word translated "unclean" here could also be translated "common." What is "common" is profane and ordinary, not consecrated and sacred. It is a consistent theme of Mark's that Jesus is like Wisdom, who, in Proverbs, goes into the marketplace to find her followers. Like Wisdom, Jesus does not shun the common and ordinary but seeks to transform it.

In 7:6-7, Jesus critiques his challengers in the language of Isaiah 29:13. In context, Isaiah is expressing God's frustration that the people of Jerusalem do not trust that God will save them from besieging enemies. God finds the root cause in the fact that the people honor him with their lips, not their hearts. Their worship has become merely routine observance of "human precepts."

In 7:8, Jesus carries this accusation even further, saying, "You disregard God's commandment but cling to human tradition." In 7:10-12, Jesus gives a concrete example of this practice. He notes how some fail to honor their parents by withholding support for them on the grounds that the money is *"qorban,"* or dedicated to God. How much this was actually done is difficult to determine. But the point of Jesus' criticism is clearly part of the larger theme of the chapter. Jesus is pointing out that human relationships are what is truly sacred, and no religious formula can rationalize that sacredness away.

tion of the elders but instead eat a meal with un-
clean hands?" 6He responded, "Well did Isaiah
prophesy about you hypocrites, as it is written:

> 'This people honors me with their lips,
> but their hearts are far from me;
> 7In vain do they worship me,
> teaching as doctrines human precepts.'

8You disregard God's commandment but cling to
human tradition." 9He went on to say, "How well
you have set aside the commandment of God in
order to uphold your tradition! 10For Moses said,
'Honor your father and your mother,' and 'Who-
ever curses father or mother shall die.' 11Yet you
say, 'If a person says to father or mother, "Any
support you might have had from me is *qorban*"'
(meaning, dedicated to God), 12you allow him to
do nothing more for his father or mother. 13You

continue

In the Pentateuch, the Hebrew word **qorban** (literally "sacrifice") is used to refer to any offering made to God and appears frequently in Leviticus and Numbers. The Greek equivalent for this term found in the Septuagint (the Greek translation of the Old Testament) is generally translated as "gift." In Jesus' time, *qorban* usually designated a vow made to consecrate property to the Temple. Such arrangements, while prohibiting the use of the donation for other uses (such as the support of parents), allowed the donor to continue to profit from the revenue generated by the property.

nullify the word of God in favor of your tradition that you have handed on. And you do many such things." [14]He summoned the crowd again and said to them, "Hear me, all of you, and understand. [15]Nothing that enters one from outside can defile that person; but the things that come out from within are what defile." [[16]]

[17]When he got home away from the crowd his disciples questioned him about the parable. [18]He said to them, "Are even you likewise without understanding? Do you not realize that everything that goes into a person from outside cannot defile, [19]since it enters not the heart but the stomach and passes out into the latrine?" (Thus he declared all foods clean.) [20]"But what comes out of a person, that is what defiles. [21]From within people, from their hearts, come evil thoughts,

continue

7:14-23 What defiles a person

Just as Mark uses a question by the Pharisees to set the stage for Jesus' teaching on what is sacred, so here he uses a question by the disciples to open up Jesus' teaching on what is defiling. Jesus says to the crowd that "Nothing that enters one from outside can defile that person" (7:15). Mark calls this a "parable" or "riddle" (7:17), indicating that it is a saying whose full meaning needs to be unpacked.

At first glance, Jesus' saying appears to challenge the Jewish dietary laws. After all, if nothing that one takes in is defiling, then why refuse to eat certain foods? The parenthetical comment "Thus he declared all foods clean" was probably added later and was intended as just such an explanation. We know, however, from Acts 10:1-16 that the question of which foods were unclean went on being debated in the early church. And as Jesus goes on teaching here, we see that he is presenting something more morally complex. The complexity is contained in what comes "from within people, from their hearts" (7:21). If we grasp the saying as a whole, we realize that the emphasis is not on dismissing what enters a person but on demonstrating the greater evil of "what comes out" (7:20). As in much of Jesus' teaching, his intent appears not so much to disregard external rules as to focus on internal realities.

7:24-30 Jesus and the Syrophoenician woman; the healing of the daughter with an unclean spirit

Mark dramatizes Jesus' point here by showing him in pagan or "unclean" territory. Here Jesus converses with a pagan woman and exorcises the unclean spirit that has possessed her daughter. In so doing, Mark is showing Jesus engaged in activities that other pious Jews of his time would have found unconventional, even shocking. Mark softens the shock value of Jesus' outreach to the Gentiles by indicating his reluctance to become involved.

First, Mark tells his audience that Jesus "wanted no one to know about" his journey to Tyre. Second, when the woman asks Jesus to cure her daughter, Mark says that Jesus first put her off by saying, "Let the children be fed first. For it is not right to take the food of the children and throw it to the dogs" (7:27). Jesus' language here indicates that he saw Israel as his priority over the Gentiles. The "children" are the children of Israel. The term "dogs" was a common and insulting way for Jews of the time to refer to Gentiles.

The woman responds in a bold and witty way by accepting these terms and turning them back to Jesus through a play on words and ideas. She says: "Lord, even the dogs under the table eat the children's scraps" (7:28). This kind of playfulness with words is typically Jewish. Mark perhaps wanted to dramatize that even someone as "unclean" as a Gentile woman with a possessed daughter was capable of parrying on equal terms with a Jew. The healing of her daughter (7:30) is linked to Mark's way of showing her, not as unclean Gentile, but as a partner in wit.

There is precedent in Hebrew Scripture for Jewish outreach to the Gentiles. In the Second Book of Kings we hear how Elisha the prophet cured the Syrian king of leprosy (2 Kgs 5:1-19).

But Mark uses language that indicates that Jesus' exchange with this woman has more meaning than a simple cure. When the woman first comes to Jesus, Mark says she heard of him "straightway"* (7:25). The word is translated above as "soon," but as we have suggested before, "straightway" is Mark's particular way of indicating moral urgency.

The words of the exchange between Jesus and the woman may also be weighted with special meaning. It was a common Jewish idiom to speak of God's word as "bread." And the word translated here as "food" is literally "bread"* (7:27), so we might understand Jesus to be saying, "It is not right to take God's word [the "bread"] and throw it to the dogs" (that is, to those who do not know how to understand it). When Mark shows Jesus conceding to the woman's wish, he may be indicating Jesus' willingness to extend God's word to the Gentiles.

A parent might do all kinds of things, stoop to all sorts of indignities, to save a child. When this Canaanite woman approaches Jesus, every generation can hear her desperation and recognize that she is literally begging for his attention to her daughter's condition. Surprisingly, Jesus not only refuses to help her but uses insulting language to make his point. But the woman brilliantly turns his metaphor around and reminds him that even dogs are entitled to scraps from the table. She turns an insult into an opportunity, and the mission of Jesus is opened wider than expected. **The Syrophoenician woman** stands in the Gospel as a kind of question mark. We might hear her asking whether our communities and families are more like those seated at table or more like those begging for scraps. Her presence also asks us to become sensitive to needs that draw us beyond familiar boundaries, and whether we are willing to make fools of ourselves to obtain what we need, or to speak out for what others need.

unchastity, theft, murder, 22adultery, greed, malice, deceit, licentiousness, envy, blasphemy, arrogance, folly. 23All these evils come from within and they defile."

The Syrophoenician Woman's Faith

24From that place he went off to the district of Tyre. He entered a house and wanted no one to know about it, but he could not escape notice. 25Soon a woman whose daughter had an unclean spirit heard about him. She came and fell at his feet. 26The woman was a Greek, a Syrophoenician by birth, and she begged him to drive the demon out of her daughter. 27He said to her, "Let the children be fed first. For it is not right to take the food of the children and throw it to the dogs." 28She replied and said to him, "Lord, even the dogs under the table eat the children's scraps." 29Then he said to her, "For saying this, you may go. The demon has gone out of your daughter." 30When the woman went home, she found the child lying in bed and the demon gone.

The Healing of a Deaf Man

31Again he left the district of Tyre and went by way of Sidon to the Sea of Galilee, into the district of the Decapolis. 32And people brought to him a deaf man who had a speech impediment and begged him to lay his hand on him. 33He took him off by himself away from the crowd. He put his

continue

7:31-37 Jesus' healing of the deaf-mute

Mark shows that Jesus continued his ministry in Gentile territory, this time on the other side of the Sea of Galilee, in Decapolis. In language that echoes the healing of the paralytic (2:3), Mark tells us that "They brought to him a man that was deaf and mute and begged him that he might lay a hand on him." Mark then describes Jesus' curing the man through a series of ritual actions known to have been used by both Greek and Jewish healers. The Aramaic phrase *ephphatha* literally means "be released,"* finger into the man's ears and, spitting, touched his tongue; [34]then he looked up to heaven and groaned, and said to him, "*Ephphatha!*" (that is, "Be opened!") [35]And [immediately] the man's ears were opened, his speech impediment was removed, and he spoke plainly. [36]He ordered them not to tell anyone. But the more he ordered them not to, the more they proclaimed it. [37]They were exceedingly astonished and they said, "He has done all things well. He makes the deaf hear and [the] mute speak."

which links it to Jesus' saying to the paralytic that his sins are released (2:5).

Mark indicates that this healing has moral significance through his use of the word "straightway"* (translated above as "immediately"): "And straightway his ears were opened and his tongue was loosed from chains and he began to speak straight"* (7:35).

By the use of the word "straightway," together with the repetition of "straight,"* Mark indicates that more is happening here than a simple cure. The whole event echoes ideas and language in Isaiah, some of which Mark showed Jesus alluding to in 4:10-13. We have noted before that when Jesus is speaking about the purpose of parables, he quotes the place in Isaiah where God says ironically:

> Make the heart of this people sluggish,
> dull their ears and close their eyes;
> Lest they see with their eyes, and hear with their ears,
> and their heart understand,
> and they turn and be healed (Isa 6:10).

And as we said earlier, of course God actually hopes the people will see and hear, understand and be healed. In a later book in Isaiah, when God is promising to save his people, God says:

> Then the eyes of the blind shall see,
> and the ears of the deaf be opened;
> Then the lame shall leap like a stag,
> and the mute tongue will sing for joy
> (Isa 35:5-6).

In this concluding episode of chapter 7, Mark shows Jesus doing what God has promised. By showing Jesus healing the deaf-mute, Mark is suggesting that Jesus is opening up people to God's word.

The **Decapolis** (meaning "ten cities") was a Gentile district of ten towns. The title is a collective one; the New Testament does not list the towns themselves (compare Mark 5:20; Matt 4:25), but they included the cities of Damascus, Sythopolis, Gadara, Gerasa, Hippos, Dion, Pella, Philadelphia, Raphana, and Canatha in the region of southern Syria and northern Jordan. These Hellenistic cities had an economic alliance that fostered their common association.

Summary of chapter 7

In this chapter, Mark develops the theme of Jesus' relationship to the "unclean. " It is a theme that Mark touched on in Jesus' first healing of the man with the unclean spirit (1:21-27); in his cure of the leper (1:40-45); in his eating with sinners (2:13-17); in the accusation that Jesus himself has an unclean spirit (3:30); in Jesus' exorcism of the Gerasene demoniac (5:2); and in the power Jesus gives his disciples to drive out unclean spirits (6:7).

This chapter has a triad structure. A homily by Jesus that redefines what makes a person "unclean" (7:14-23) is framed by two conversations on the subject. Before the homily, Jesus has a conversation with men of traditional piety about what is sacred and what is "unclean" or profane (7:1-14). After the homily, he has an unconventional dialogue with a pagan woman and drives out an unclean spirit from her daughter (7:24-30). Mark shows Jesus responding to the challenge of those who think in conventional terms by redefining what is "unclean." Mark dramatizes this redefinition by showing Jesus' outreach to the Gentile woman and her daughter.

In the concluding episode Mark indicates the significance of Jesus' redefinition by showing him engaged in healing a deaf-mute, an action that symbolizes the opening of people's ears to the meaning of God's word.

EXPLORING LESSON FOUR

1. How has familiarity with Jesus and his family affected the response to him by people of his hometown (6:1-3)? (See also Luke 4:16-30.) When have you been surprised by the character or qualities of an adult you knew since childhood?

2. Jesus sent the Twelve out to share in his mission (6:6b-16). At our baptism we are each called to share in Jesus' mission. In what ways have you sensed this call?

3. a) Why did Herod imprison John the Baptist (6:17-20)?

   b) What prophetic voices have you recognized as courageously speaking truth to power? In what ways have they suffered for it?

4. a) Why has Jesus told his disciples to come with him to a deserted place (6:30-32)?

   b) When do you find yourself in need of spiritual renewal? Where or how are you most likely to find it?

5. What are some of the eucharistic themes you see in Mark's account of the feeding of the five thousand (6:34-44)? (See also Mark 14:22-25.)

6. What are some other biblical circumstances where God's people have been told: "Do not be afraid" (6:50)? (See Gen 46:2-4; Exod 20:20; 1 Kgs 17:8-14; Isa 43:1-5; Matt 1:18-20; Luke 12:6-30.)

7. What spiritual practices might strengthen our interior lives, protecting us from the kind of defilement Jesus says can spring from within a person (7:14-23)? (See also Phil 4:8-9; Col 3:16.)

8. Why did Jesus initially resist the Syrophoenician woman's request to rid her daughter of a demon (7:25-30)? (See Matt 15:22-28.) What changed his mind?

9. In healing the deaf-mute, Jesus called for his ears to be "opened" (7:34). Recall a time when you felt your ears were truly opened to hear the word or voice of God.

CLOSING PRAYER

"They had not understood the incident of the loaves." (Mark 6:52)

Give us eyes, Lord, that not only see but perceive, and ears that not only hear but understand. Count us among those who are eagerly growing in understanding so that we may walk more closely with you. We pray this day for those who, along with each of us, are in need of this grace . . .

LESSON FIVE

Mark 8:1–9:32

Begin your personal study and group discussion with a simple and sincere prayer such as:

Prayer

Loving God, open my mind and heart to hear your voice. Increase my understanding and inspire in me a greater desire to follow Jesus.

Read the Bible text of Mark 8:1–9:32 found in the outside columns of pages 76–86, highlighting what stands out to you.

Read the accompanying commentary to add to your understanding.

Respond to the questions on pages 87–88, Exploring Lesson Five.

The Closing Prayer on page 89 is for your personal use and may be used at the end of group discussion.

CHAPTER 8

The Feeding of Four Thousand

[1]In those days when there again was a great crowd without anything to eat, he summoned the disciples and said, [2]"My heart is moved with pity for the crowd, because they have been with me now for three days and have nothing to eat. [3]If I send them away hungry to their homes, they will collapse on the way, and some of them have come a great distance." [4]His disciples answered him, "Where can anyone get enough bread to satisfy them here in this deserted place?" [5]Still he asked them, "How many loaves do you have?" "Seven," they replied. [6]He ordered the crowd to sit down on the ground. Then, taking the seven loaves he gave thanks, broke them, and gave them to his disciples to distribute, and they distributed them to the crowd. [7]They also had a few fish. He said the blessing over them and ordered them distributed also. [8]They ate and were satisfied. They picked up the fragments left over—seven baskets. [9]There were about four thousand people.

He dismissed them [10]and got into the boat with his disciples and came to the region of Dalmanutha.

continue

SECOND SIGHT—A SHARPER FOCUS

Mark 8:1-38

8:1-10 The second feeding of a crowd

Mark designs his Gospel so that themes, images, and even events are repeated more than once. With hindsight the reader becomes aware of a pattern of doublets. There is a theological purpose to this design that chapter 8 points to, which we will discuss later. The doublet at the beginning of chapter 8 is striking: once again a large and hungry crowd is gathered around Jesus, and once again he feeds them with scant supplies. Once again there are baskets left over. (Compare 6:34-44.)

There are also some interesting details of difference. In the first scenario, Jesus is "moved with pity" for the crowd because they "were like sheep without a shepherd" (6:34); his initial compassion is for their spiritual hunger. Here Jesus is concerned about the crowd because they have been with him "for three days and have nothing to eat" (8:2). In the first scene, the disciples approach Jesus about the situation (6:35); here Jesus approaches them (8:1-3). In the first scene, they distribute "five loaves and two fish" (6:38); here they distribute seven loaves and "a few fish" (8:6-7). In both instances, Jesus orders the crowd to sit down to be fed, but in the first one he suggests that they form meal-sharing groups (6:39), a detail that is omitted here. In both instances Jesus prays over the bread and then breaks it, but in the first scene Mark specifically says that he "said the blessing" over it (6:41), while in the second, Mark says he "gave thanks" (8:6). In both cases, Mark tells us that the people ate "and were satisfied" (6:42; 8:8). In both scenes, the disciples gather up baskets of leftovers, but in the first instance it is twelve (6:43), while in the second there are seven (8:8).

Is there any significance to these small differences? Many scholars have suggested that the first feeding is suggestive of God feeding his people with manna, while the second is suggestive of the Eucharist. To arrive at this conclusion, they note that the "three days" of chapter 8 suggests Jesus' three days in the tomb; that saying a blessing over the bread is the conventional description of the Jewish grace before meals, while the giving of thanks over it suggests the Eucharist (which literally means "thanksgiving"); that the number twelve in the first episode suggests the twelve tribes of Israel, while the number seven suggests the sacraments of the church. Yet there are many flaws in these arguments: "three days" was a conventional biblical way of indicating a long period of time; the Jewish blessing over food is in fact a prayer of thanksgiving; and the sacraments of the church were not numbered for many centuries. So it would seem that to call the first miracle Jewish and the second one Christian is strained. What is clear is that Mark wanted his audience to be aware of a miraculous event that repeated itself.

The Demand for a Sign

[11]The Pharisees came forward and began to argue with him, seeking from him a sign from heaven to test him. [12]He sighed from the depth of his spirit and said, "Why does this generation seek a sign? Amen, I say to you, no sign will be given to this generation." [13]Then he left them, got into the boat again, and went off to the other shore.

The Leaven of the Pharisees

[14]They had forgotten to bring bread, and they had only one loaf with them in the boat. [15]He enjoined them, "Watch out, guard against the leaven of the Pharisees and the leaven of Herod." [16]They concluded among themselves that it was because they had no bread. [17]When he became aware of this he said to them, "Why do you conclude that it is because you have no bread? Do you not yet understand or comprehend? Are your hearts hardened? [18]Do you have eyes and not see, ears and not hear? And do you not remember, [19]when I broke the five loaves for the five thousand, how many wicker baskets full of fragments you picked up?" They answered him, "Twelve." [20]"When I broke the seven loaves for the four thousand, how many full baskets of fragments did you pick up?" They answered [him], "Seven." [21]He said to them, "Do you still not understand?"

continue

8:11-21 Double failures to understand

What follows are two episodes in which first the Pharisees and then Jesus' disciples fail to get the point of the miracle he has just performed. Although they are usually treated separately, it is important to see that they are designed to be parallel. They are also equal in irony.

If one is reading the Gospel as a literal account, one could, of course, shrug off the Pharisees' request for "a sign from heaven" (8:11) by saying that there is no reason to think that the Pharisees were present at the miraculous feeding. But if one agrees that Mark has a theological design, then one perceives the juxtaposition of the feeding miracle and the Pharisees' request for "a sign from heaven" as Mark's way of indicating the Pharisees' obtuseness. When Mark goes on to say that Jesus' response was to sigh "from the depth of his spirit" (8:12), the reader shares that sense of exasperation.

The episode that follows (8:14-23) shows that the disciples have a parallel obtuseness. Mark dramatizes this in several ways. First, he quotes Jesus warning them against "the leaven of the Pharisees and the leaven of Herod" (8:15). Conventionally, "leaven" was considered to be a symbol of puffery or pride, so Jesus is apparently cautioning them against being too self-sufficient to trust in God. The disciples' response misses the point completely. Taking his words literally, "They concluded among themselves that it was because they had no bread" (8:16).

In describing how Jesus reproached them, Mark uses words that repeat earlier moments in the Gospel. At the end of chapter 6, when the disciples are frightened by seeing Jesus walk on the water and still the storm (6:49-51), Mark tells us, "They had not understood the incident of the loaves. On the contrary, their hearts were hardened" (6:52). So here, when

The Blind Man of Bethsaida

[22]When they arrived at Bethsaida, they brought to him a blind man and begged him to touch him. [23]He took the blind man by the hand and led him outside the village. Putting spittle on his eyes he laid his hands on him and asked, "Do you see anything?" [24]Looking up he replied, "I see people looking like trees and walking." [25]Then he laid hands on his eyes a second time and he saw clearly; his sight was restored and he could see everything distinctly. [26]Then he sent him home and said, "Do not even go into the village."

continue

Mark shows Jesus saying, "Why do you conclude you have no bread? Do you not yet understand or comprehend? Are your hearts hardened? . . . And do you not remember when I broke the five loaves for the five thousand . . . ?" (8:17-19), we hear a repetition of that earlier moment when the disciples missed the point. The repetition serves to underline the disciples' obtuseness.

8:22-26 The two-stage healing of the blind man

Like the healing of the deaf-mute at the end of chapter 7, the healing of the blind man here has symbolic significance. Particular elements of that earlier healing are repeated here. In both instances, Mark tells us that Jesus took the person aside (7:33; 8:23); in both, Mark indicates a laying on of hands (7:32; 8:25); in both, Mark says that Jesus used spittle as a means of healing (7:33; 8:23). The repeating details are enough to alert the reader to the fact that one healing is linked to the other. On a deeper level, they are linked in terms of the context of Isaiah:

> Then will the eyes of the blind shall see,
> the ears of the deaf be opened;
> Then shall the lame leap like a stag,
> and the mute tongue sing for joy
> (Isa 35:5-6).

In the earlier healing, Mark shows Jesus clearing the ears of the deaf and opening his mouth; here he shows Jesus opening the eyes of the blind.

The episode here also sheds light on Mark's structural habit of repeating incidents. The blind man does not see clearly right away; it takes a second laying on of hands before he "could see everything distinctly" (8:25). In the same way, Mark repeats incidents so that the reader can see more readily what he is about. So he describes two episodes that show Jesus is in command of the sea (4:35-41; 6:45-52); he twice describes Jesus miraculously feeding the people in the desert; he offers two healing incidents that dramatize how Jesus enacts the words of Isaiah.

This kind of structure may be related to the structure of Hebrew verse, which often repeats an initial thought in varied words. In Psalm 19, for example, we read:

> The law of the LORD is perfect,
> refreshing the soul.
> The decree of the LORD is trustworthy,
> giving wisdom to the simple (Ps 19:8).

Bethsaida in the region of Galilee

The second verse repeats but varies the idea of the first, thereby enriching it. One commentator has described this structure as giving us "A, and what's more, B." In the same way, Mark's second, repeating episodes vary and enrich the significance of the first, making us grasp their meaning more clearly. In Part Two of this study, we will discuss the way in which the whole second half of Mark's Gospel (chs. 9–16) functions as a second verse, clarifying and enriching the teachings and actions of Jesus in the first half (chs. 1–8).

8:27-33 A second discussion of the identity of Jesus

The question that Mark shows Jesus raising here, "Who do people say that I am?" (8:27), is also a repetition. We have heard it before, although indirectly. In chapter 6, Mark tells us that people are talking about who Jesus is and offering various opinions: "John the Baptist has been raised from the dead . . . . He is Elijah . . . . He is a prophet like any of the prophets" (6:14-15). When Mark gives the disciples' response to Jesus' question here, he shows them repeating these opinions verbatim: "They said in reply, 'John the Baptist, others Elijah, still others one of the prophets' " (8:28). Mark then shows Jesus asking the question directly of his disciples (8:29).

The response that Mark shows Peter making—"You are the Messiah" (8:29)—is strikingly different from the other speculations. Most Christians accept that response in the light of their own faith today. They also tend to perceive it through the lens of Matthew, who first adds to Peter's confession, "the Son of the living God" (Matt 16:16), and who then shows Jesus responding, "Blessed are you, Simon son of Jonah. For flesh and blood has not revealed this to you, but my heavenly Father. And so I say to you, you are Peter, and upon this rock I will build my church" (Matt 16:17-18). But readers who see the four evangelists as four different theologians will be sensitive to the different nuances in Mark's dramatization of what happens next.

In Mark's version, Jesus does not commend Peter for his reply. Instead, he charges the disciples not to speak about him (8:30) and goes on to tell them, for the first time, how he will suffer, die, and be raised up again (8:31). Mark then describes Peter as so unable to accept this prediction that he "rebuke[s]" Jesus (8:32). Although Mark does not spell it out, the implication seems to be that Peter cannot accept the idea of Jesus' suffering and death; it does not fit his idea of a "messiah." Mark indicates that Jesus, in turn, cannot accept Peter's interpretation of who he is and that he rebukes him in radically strong language: "Get behind me, Satan. You are thinking not as God does, but as human beings do" (8:33).

Matthew also describes this second exchange between Jesus and Peter, but only after Jesus has commended Peter and told him that he will found his church upon him. What are we to make of this radical difference? If one is reading the Gospels as literal eyewitness ac-

III: The Mystery Begins to Be Revealed

Peter's Confession about Jesus

27 Now Jesus and his disciples set out for the villages of Caesarea Philippi. Along the way he asked his disciples, "Who do people say that I am?" 28 They said in reply, "John the Baptist, others Elijah, still others one of the prophets." 29 And he asked them, "But who do you say that I am?" Peter said to him in reply, "You are the Messiah." 30 Then he warned them not to tell anyone about him.

The First Prediction of the Passion

31 He began to teach them that the Son of Man must suffer greatly and be rejected by the elders, the chief priests, and the scribes, and be killed, and rise after three days. 32 He spoke this openly. Then Peter took him aside and began to rebuke him. 33 At this he turned around and, looking at his disciples, rebuked Peter and said, "Get behind me, Satan. You are thinking not as God does, but as human beings do."

continue

The Conditions of Discipleship

34He summoned the crowd with his disciples and said to them, "Whoever wishes to come after me must deny himself, take up his cross, and follow me. 35For whoever wishes to save his life will lose it, but whoever loses his life for my sake and that of the gospel will save it. 36What profit is there for one to gain the whole world and forfeit his life? 37What could one give in exchange for his life? 38Whoever is ashamed of me and of my words in this faithless and sinful generation, the Son of Man will be ashamed of when he comes in his Father's glory with the holy angels."

continue

counts, one must resort to examining sources and speculating on how one evangelist took from one source and the other from another. But if one is reading the Gospels as theology (which the church now encourages us to do), one concludes that Mark had a different theological interpretation of this event than Matthew. Since Mark's is the earliest Gospel, one might then conclude that Mark and Matthew were each responding to the theological needs of their own time and respective faith-communities. In Matthew's time (probably a decade later than Mark's), the Christian community was beginning to emerge as a church. (Indeed, the word is used for the first time here in Matthew 16.) Moreover, it was undergoing persecution and needed to be affirmed as a community under God's care. In Mark's time, the Jesus-community saw itself as part of Judaism. The pressing issue was not, therefore, God's providence (which would have been taken for granted), but why Jesus was so important to them and what they meant in calling him "Messiah."

Contrary to popular belief, recent scholarship has shown that there was no single, fixed concept of "the Messiah" within Judaism of the first century. The term, which in Hebrew simply means "the anointed one," was used variably, both in the Hebrew Bible and in other Jewish writings that were contemporaneous with Jesus and Mark. Within the Hebrew Bible, it is most often applied to a king, but also to a high priest or a patriarch. Isaiah applied it to the Persian king Cyrus, who allowed the Jews to go home to Jerusalem from captivity in Babylon (Isa 45:1). In the Jewish writings outside the Bible, the term is variously applied to a teacher, a warrior, and a judge. The Dead Sea Scrolls anticipated the coming of two messiahs, a king and a high priest. In short, one cannot pin the term down to a particular definition but must acknowledge that it was generally used to indicate any figure whom the faith-community saw as God's representative, someone who was doing God's work on its behalf.

The one constant in all these variations was that a "messiah," as God's agent, was always imagined as victorious in his work. When Mark shows Peter rebuking Jesus for telling them he would die, he is showing Peter reacting on the basis of this assumption of victory and triumph. By the same token, when Mark shows Jesus rebuking Peter, he is indicating that Jesus was rebuking him for this assumption. Nowhere in Judaism before Jesus is there evidence of a suffering messiah. (Isaiah's "Suffering Servant" [Isa 52:13–53:12] was not considered messianic.) Only after Christianity was established did the idea begin to develop within Judaism. Here it is Peter's rejection of a suffering messiah that Jesus labels human-minded and not God-minded (8:33).

8:34-38 The second commissioning of Jesus' disciples

Mark shows that in the first commissioning of his disciples, Jesus sends them out to imitate him in preaching repentance, driving out demons, and curing the sick (6:7-13). We noted earlier that when Mark interleaves the story of John the Baptist between this commissioning and the disciples' return from their first efforts (6:14-29), he subtly suggests the destiny of both Jesus and Jesus' disciples. The death of John the Baptist is a foreshadowing of Jesus' death. Since Jesus has just instructed his disciples to imitate him, the placement of John's narrative at this point suggests that they will also be called to imitate him in the yielding of their lives. Here in chapter 8 this indirect suggestion is made clear. Mark shows us Jesus speaking plainly about what is involved in being his disciple: "Whoever wishes to come after me must deny himself, take up his cross, and follow me" (8:34).

The chapter concludes with Mark indicating that death, however, is not the end of the story. He has just shown Jesus asserting the paradox that "Whoever wishes to save his life will lose it, but whoever loses his life for my sake and that of the gospel will save it" (8:35). Mark develops the implications of this paradox by indicating that at the end of time, Jesus will determine his followers accordingly: "Whoever is ashamed of me . . . the Son of Man will be ashamed of when he comes in his Father's glory with the holy angels" (8:38). Some would like to read "son of man" here as the title of triumphant, apocalyptic figure, but as in 2:10, it makes sense to read it instead as the Aramaic form of self-reference. The use of the word "ashamed" emphasizes the fact that the cross is not only a painful death but a shameful one, and the followers of Jesus need to be prepared for worldly shame as well as physical suffering. Yet Mark also shows how Jesus implied that the shame of the cross would one day be replaced by the glory of the Father's presence. Mark thus prepares the reader for the transfiguration of Jesus, which follows in chapter 9.

The section between Mark 8:22 and 10:52 is a large narrative devoted to the theme of **discipleship**. It is framed by two stories of blind men whose faith contrasts with that of the disciples (8:22-26; 10:46-52). Whereas they learn to "see," Jesus' disciples remain "blind" to Jesus' true mission as the suffering son of man, the messiah.

Summary of chapter 8

In this chapter, Mark repeats some earlier events, images, and ideas. In doing so, he does not present exact repetitions but offers variations on the theme. It is a chapter of doublets. The chapter opens with a second episode in which Jesus feeds a great crowd in a deserted place. It is followed by the double misunderstanding of the miracle both by the Pharisees and by the disciples. It concludes with a second discussion of Jesus' identity and with a second commissioning of his disciples. In describing the disciples' failure to understand, Mark shows Jesus asking, "Are your hearts hardened?" (8:17) thus echoing the language of Jesus' dismay in chapter 6.

In presenting a second discussion of Jesus' identity and a second commissioning of the disciples, Mark sharpens the readers' focus. In the earlier discussions of chapter 6, Mark only hints that suffering and death will be significant parts of their destiny. Mark's main focus is on Jesus' power to heal and restore and on his passing on this power to his disciples. The emphasis is on Jesus as a miracle-worker and his disciples as potentially like him.

In chapter 8, however, Mark reverses the emphasis and begins to show that Jesus sees himself and his disciples as destined for a shameful death. Mark has shown Jesus speaking in parables and riddling sayings before. Here he shows him offering the ultimate paradox of losing one's life in order to save it.

This shift and sharpening of focus is symbolized in the two-stage healing of the blind man, itself a variation on the symbolic healing of the deaf-mute in chapter 7. Both healings take their meaning from the passage in Isaiah where God promises the ultimate healing and restoration of his people. Beyond that, the healing of the blind man has special significance because of the way Mark tells the story. By dramatizing the cure of the blind man in two stages, Mark indicates the theological purpose of his structure of doublets. The second time around, Mark strives to make the meaning of Jesus clearer. In the same way, the whole second half of Mark's Gospel (chs. 9–16) serves to clarify the first. The

CHAPTER 9

[1]He also said to them, "Amen, I say to you, there are some standing here who will not taste death until they see that the kingdom of God has come in power."

The Transfiguration of Jesus

[2]After six days Jesus took Peter, James, and John and led them up a high mountain apart by themselves. And he was transfigured before them, [3]and his clothes became dazzling white, such as no fuller on earth could bleach them. [4]Then Elijah appeared to them along with Moses, and they were conversing with Jesus. [5]Then Peter said to Jesus in reply, "Rabbi, it is good that we are here! Let us make three tents: one for you, one for Moses, and one for Elijah." [6]He hardly knew what to say, they were so terrified. [7]Then a cloud came, casting a shadow over them; then from the cloud came a voice, "This is my beloved Son. Listen to him."

continue

hinge between the two lies here at the end of chapter 8. When Mark shows Jesus speaking of a time of future glory, he prepares the reader for the scene of Jesus' transfiguration.

TRANSFIGURATION— NEW PERCEPTIONS

Mark 9:1-32

9:1-7 The Transfiguration

Mark opens this chapter by quoting Jesus' promise that some of those around him will see the kingdom of God before they die (9:1). This assertion is often interpreted to mean that Jesus promised that the end of the world would come soon, or at least that the first followers of Jesus believed that was to happen. But such an interpretation comes from reading the text as a literal account. If instead one sees Mark's shaping hand here, one sees that he was preparing his readers for the transfiguration scene that comes immediately afterward. The transfiguration does in fact present an imaginative rendering of what God's final kingdom will be like.

The word that is conventionally translated "transfigured" is actually "metamorphosed,"* which indicates not just a change in appearance but a changed state of being. There is a sense of new beginnings. The time frame of "six days" (9:2) is suggestive of the six days of Creation before God's Sabbath rest. Mark intensifies the sense of a new creation when he describes God's voice saying to Jesus the very same words he spoke at the moment of his baptism (compare 9:7 with 1:11).

The reference to "six days" also recalls the period Moses waited before the divine voice called to him on the mountain of Sinai (Exod 24:12-18). Mark further links Jesus to Moses by describing Jesus talking with him. It is significant that Jesus is pictured conversing with the two greatest figures of Jewish tradition, Moses and Elijah (9:4), representatives of the Law and the Prophets. Jesus, whom Mark has shown to be God's Wisdom, is in conversation with the traditional figures of Jewish wisdom. It is a timeless moment. Mark emphasizes that he sees Jesus as one of them. He perceives Jesus to be a continuation of the wisdom of Israel.

This trio of great figures is matched by a trio of disciples. They are the same three disciples Mark shows Jesus taking with him to witness the raising up of the little girl (5:37); they will be the same three that Mark will show Jesus taking with him into the garden of Gethsemane (14:33). In terms of Markan structure, these episodes form a triad, and the middle or key incident is here in chapter 9. By noting that Jesus took them "up a high mountain" and "apart" (9:2), Mark indicates that Jesus is trying to lead them into his transfigured state. And as Mark describes the scene, they, too, for a brief moment, are changed.

Peter's desire to build three tents (or "booths"*) may seem puzzling unless one is aware of the Jewish feast of Booths (or "Tabernacles"). It is a feast that follows the Jewish New Year and is intended to celebrate the natural harvest as a sign of God's final harvest. It is a feast of the end time. It takes its name from the fact that it is observed by the construction of temporary outdoor huts or "booths," which are decorated with the fruits of the harvest. When Mark shows Peter wanting to build three booths here, he is indicating Peter's perception that he has entered the end time of God's final kingdom.

Unfortunately, this meaning of Peter's question is obscured by the translation "tents." It is also canceled out by the conventional translation, "He hardly knew what to say, they were so terrified" (9:6). The word translated as "terrified" here would be better translated "filled with awe."* If it were, one would hear the echo of the end of chapter 4, where the disciples ask each other, "Who then is this whom even wind and sea obey?" (4:41). That Mark intends to signal awe rather than fright is indicated by the first statement he shows Peter saying: "Rabbi, it is good that we are here!" (9:5). A feeling of goodness is compatible with awe but not with terror. Mark's suggestion that Peter was overwhelmed by the goodness of God's presence is also his way of indicating that Peter, too, has been transfigured, however briefly. As Jesus' transfiguration looks forward to his resurrection, so Peter's state here gives promise of his future glory.

The words Mark uses to describe Jesus' clothing are suggestive of the prophet Malachi's description of God's messenger when he comes at the end of time to judge, purify, and gather God's people (Mal 3:1-3). In that passage God says:

> Now I am sending my messenger—
> he will prepare the way before me;
> And the lord whom you seek will come
> suddenly to his temple;
> The messenger of the covenant whom you desire—
> see, he is coming! says the LORD of hosts.
> But who can endure the day of his coming?
> Who can stand firm when he appears?
> For he will be like a refiner's fire,
> like fullers' lye.
> He will sit refining and purifying silver,
> and he will purify the Levites,
> Refining them like gold or silver,
> that they may bring offerings to the LORD in
> righteousness.

As we noted at the time, Mark alludes briefly to this passage in the very opening of his Gospel (1:2). Here he comes back to it by describing Jesus' garments as "dazzling white, such as no fuller on earth could bleach them" (9:3). By emphasizing that Jesus' clothing is whiter than the "fullers' lye," Mark links him to Malachi's prophet of the end time.

A **theophany** is an extraordinary, visible appearance of God in the physical world. Such appearances are revelations of the divine. The transfiguration of Jesus shares many of the attributes of theophanies recounted in the Old Testament, especially that of Sinai (Exod 19:16-19; 24:15-18; 34:29-30; 40:34-38). Many of the motifs seen in the Sinai theophany are also present in Jesus' transfiguration: the overshadowing cloud, the mountain setting, and the sense of awe that overwhelms the witnesses. Moreover, just as the theophany on Sinai served as a channel of communication between God and the Israelites, the theophany of the transfiguration is an occasion for God to speak directly to human beings: "This is my beloved Son. Listen to him" (Mark 9:7). Jesus' personal transformation suggests a revelation of his own divinity, as his changed appearance recalls that of the "Ancient of Days" in Daniel 7:9: "His clothing was white as snow, / the hair on his head like pure wool." This depiction of Jesus is encountered again in Revelation 1:14.

8Suddenly, looking around, they no longer saw anyone but Jesus alone with them.

The Coming of Elijah

9As they were coming down from the mountain, he charged them not to relate what they had seen to anyone, except when the Son of Man had risen from the dead. 10So they kept the matter to themselves, questioning what rising from the dead meant. 11Then they asked him, "Why do the scribes say that Elijah must come first?" 12He told them, "Elijah will indeed come first and restore all things, yet how is it written regarding the Son of Man that he must suffer greatly and be treated with contempt? 13But I tell you that Elijah has come and they did to him whatever they pleased, as it is written of him."

The Healing of a Boy with a Demon

14When they came to the disciples, they saw a large crowd around them and scribes arguing with them. 15Immediately on seeing him, the whole crowd was utterly amazed. They ran up to him and greeted him. 16He asked them, "What are you arguing about with them?" 17Someone from the crowd answered him, "Teacher, I have brought to you my son possessed by a mute spirit. 18Wherever it seizes him, it throws him down; he foams at the mouth, grinds his teeth, and becomes rigid. I asked your disciples to drive it out, but they were

continue

9:8-10 The descent from the mountain

The vision of future glory fades abruptly: "Suddenly, looking around, they no longer saw anyone but Jesus alone with them" (9:8). Jesus charges them not to tell what they have seen until after he has risen from the dead (9:9). And these disciples, who were the very ones to witness Jesus' raising up of the little girl (5:37), question one another about the meaning of the term "rising from the dead" (9:10). Their descent from the mountain is not only physical but spiritual. They have returned from a brief moment of insight to their usual state of dulled understanding.

9:11-13 Elijah

Elijah is a recurring figure in Mark's Gospel. As we noted earlier, Mark describes John the Baptist in a way that makes him resemble Elijah (1:6). Biblical legend had it that Elijah never died but was taken up to heaven in a fiery chariot (2 Kgs 2:11) and would return some day to prepare God's people for the end time (Mal 3:23). In chapter 6, Mark tells us that people speculated that Jesus might be Elijah come back (6:15). In chapter 8, he indicates that some of the disciples thought the same (8:28). But in the transfiguration scene, Mark shows Jesus talking with Elijah, thus suggesting that Jesus is compatible with Elijah and yet distinct from him.

As further clarification, Mark shows an exchange about Elijah between Jesus and his disciples. The disciples ask why Elijah had to come first (that is, before the end time). Jesus' response falls into three parts. First he echoes the prophecy of Malachi that Elijah has to come "and restore all things" (9:12). Then he turns the question about and asks why he himself ("the son of man") has to suffer. Finally he declares that "Elijah has come and they did to him whatever they pleased" (9:13).

There are gaps in this reply. Nonetheless, Mark seems to be using it to clarify both the similarities and dissimilarities between Jesus and Elijah. First he shows Jesus acknowledging Elijah as a forerunner. At the same time, he shows Jesus comparing his own sufferings to come with those of Elijah.

The reference to Elijah's suffering makes no sense in terms of the narratives concerning Elijah in the Second Book of Kings. The reference only makes sense as an identification of Elijah with John the Baptist. So the exchange serves to confirm what Mark has been doing throughout his Gospel: he has identified John the Baptist with Elijah and shown him to be the forerunner of Jesus, not only in his drawing people to God but also in his unjust suffering and death.

We suggested earlier that in chapter 6 Mark inserts the story of John the Baptist's death into the narrative of the disciples' mission as a subtle forewarning of what they themselves should expect (6:19-29). Here Mark makes the connection clear.

9:14-29 The healing of the boy with a mute and deaf spirit

This healing recapitulates and incorporates a number of healings that Mark has shown Jesus performing in the first half of the Gospel. The exorcism of a "mute and deaf spirit" (9:25) recalls the healing of the deaf-mute in 7:33-37. The violently destructive effects of the unclean spirit (9:18-26) are reminiscent of the demonic possession of the man among the tombs in 5:1-20. Jesus' "rebuke" of the spirit (9:25) echoes his first exorcism of the man in the synagogue (1:25). The corpse-like appearance of the boy and the bystanders' insistence that "He is dead" (9:26) recall the apparent death of Jairus's daughter (5:38-43). And Jesus' gesture of taking the boy by the hand and raising him up (9:27) repeats Jesus' way of raising that little girl and bringing her back to life (5:41). The attentive reader has a sense of déjà vu.

Mark does not simply provide a repetitive incident, however. He adds to it a whole discussion of how unclean spirits can be driven out. Mark tells us first that the crowd, some scribes, and the disciples were all arguing about it (9:14). He notes that the disciples, although commissioned by Jesus to drive out demons (6:7), have failed in this instance. He shows the disciples asking Jesus why they have failed (9:28), and he provides Jesus' answer as the climax to the episode: "This kind can only come out through prayer" (9:29).

Accordingly, Mark places great emphasis here on the importance of faith as part of the healing process. He shows Jesus sighing over the disciples' lack of faith (9:19). He gives Jesus' reply to the boy's father: "Everything is possible to one who has faith" (9:23). He dramatizes the father praying, "I do believe; help my unbelief!" (9:24).

In the first part of his Gospel, Mark shows Jesus performing one miracle after another easily and, as it were, automatically. But here he indicates that miracles are not automatic events; rather, he indicates that healings are a process that involves faith and prayer.

unable to do so." 19He said to them in reply, "O faithless generation, how long will I be with you? How long will I endure you? Bring him to me." 20They brought the boy to him. And when he saw him, the spirit immediately threw the boy into convulsions. As he fell to the ground, he began to roll around and foam at the mouth. 21Then he questioned his father, "How long has this been happening to him?" He replied, "Since childhood. 22It has often thrown him into fire and into water to kill him. But if you can do anything, have compassion on us and help us." 23Jesus said to him, "'If you can!' Everything is possible to one who has faith." 24Then the boy's father cried out, "I do believe, help my unbelief!" 25Jesus, on seeing a crowd rapidly gathering, rebuked the unclean spirit and said to it, "Mute and deaf spirit, I command you: come out of him and never enter him again!" 26Shouting and throwing the boy into convulsions, it came out. He became like a corpse, which caused many to say, "He is dead!" 27But Jesus took him by the hand, raised him, and he stood up. 28When he entered the house, his disciples asked him in private, "Why could we not drive it out?" 29He said to them, "This kind can only come out through prayer."

The Second Prediction of the Passion

30They left from there and began a journey through Galilee, but he did not wish anyone to know about it. 31He was teaching his disciples and

continue

9:30-32 Jesus' second prediction of his death and resurrection

This prediction is the middle of a triad of predictions. The first occurs in 8:31; the third will occur in 10:33-34. The language is almost identical in each case, but not quite. In the first prediction, Mark shows Jesus speaking of telling them, "The Son of Man is to be handed over to men and they will kill him, and three days after his death he will rise." 32But they did not understand the saying, and they were afraid to question him.

being rejected "by the elders, the chief priests, and the scribes" and then being killed. The passive voice used here does not indicate the agent of the killing. In the third prediction, Mark shows Jesus telling his disciples that he will be "handed over to the chief priests and the scribes" who will, in turn, "hand him over to the Gentiles" who will put him to death. In this middle and key version, Mark quotes Jesus as saying that he will be "handed over to [human beings] and they will kill him." In this key version, Mark suggests that all humanity rather than a particular agent is responsible for Jesus' death. Mark makes a point of saying that the disciples do not understand (9:32).

EXPLORING LESSON FIVE

1. What importance do you see in the differences between Mark's accounts of the feeding of the five thousand (6:34-44) and the feeding of the four thousand (8:1-10)?

2. Why might the Pharisees' demand for a sign so deeply disturb Jesus (8:12-13)? (See Matt 12:39-40; Luke 23:8-9; 1 Cor 1:21-23.) When are you tempted to ask for some supernatural sign?

3. The disciples have seen the signs Jesus performed in feeding the multitudes, yet they fail to understand Jesus and his mission (8:14-21). What nourishment has God provided in your life that helps sustain your faith in Jesus?

4. Jesus asks his disciples, "Do you have eyes and not see . . . ?" (8:18). Shortly thereafter, Mark tells of Jesus restoring sight to a blind man in two stages (8:22-26). What connection might there be between this healing and the disciples' failure to see?

5. Who do *you* say Jesus is (8:27)? How would you identify him or describe him?

6. Jesus rebukes Peter, calling him "Satan" (8:31-33) shortly after Peter has called Jesus "the Messiah" (8:27-30). What might this say about Peter's expectations of Jesus as the Messiah?

7. What are some of the crosses you have had to bear in life (8:34-38)? How has being a follower of Christ made a difference in how you have carried them?

8. Explain the feast of Booths and its significance in Mark 9:5. (See Lev 23:33-43; Neh 8:14-18.)

9. How has Elijah already come (9:13)? (See Mal 3:23-24; Luke 1:17.)

10. What is significant about the wording Jesus uses in the second prediction of his passion (9:31)?

CLOSING PRAYER

"But who do you say that I am?" (Mark 8:29)

Jesus, Messiah, confirm in us your identity as God's anointed. Point us toward a rich understanding of your role in our personal lives and in our world. As we bear witness to you, we ask for help in bearing these crosses which we now lift up in prayer . . .

PRAYING WITH YOUR GROUP

Because we know that the Bible allows us to hear God's voice, prayer provides the context for our study and sharing. By speaking and listening to God and each other, the discussion often grows to more deeply bond us to one another and to God.

At *the beginning and end of each lesson* simple prayers are provided for individual use, and also may be used within the group setting. Most of the closing prayers provided with each lesson relate directly to a theme from that lesson and encourage you to pray together for people and events in your local community.

Of course, there are many ways to center ourselves in God's presence as we gather together in groups around the word of God. We provide some additional suggestions here knowing you and your group will make prayer a priority as part of your gathering. These are simply alternative ways to pray if your group would like to try something different from those prayers provided in the previous pages.

Conversational Prayer

This form of prayer allows for the group members to pray in their own words in a way that is not intimidating. The group leader begins with Step One, inviting all to focus on the presence of Christ among them. After a few moments of quiet, the group leader invites anyone in the group to voice a prayer or two of thanksgiving; once that is complete, then anyone who has personal intentions may pray in their own words for their needs; finally, the group prays for the needs of others.

A suggested process:
In your own words, speak simple and short prayers to allow time for others to add their voices.

Focus on one "step" at a time, not worrying about praying for everything in your mental list at once.

Step One	Visualize Christ. Welcome him. Imagine him present with you in your group. Allow time for some silence.
Step Two	Gratitude opens our hearts. Use simple words such as, "Thank you, Lord, for . . ."
Step Three	Pray for your own needs knowing that others will pray with you. Be specific and honest. Use "I" and "me" language.

Step Four	Pray for others by name, with love. You may voice your agreement ("Yes, Lord"). End with gratitude for sharing concerns.

Praying Like Ignatius

St. Ignatius Loyola, whose life and ministry are the foundation of the Jesuit community, invites us to enter into Scripture texts in order to experience the scenes, especially scenes of the gospels or other narrative parts of Scripture. Simply put, this is a method of creatively imagining the scene, viewing it from the inside, and asking God to meet you there. Most often, this is a personal form of prayer, but in a group setting, some of its elements can be helpful if you allow time for this process.

A suggested process:

- Select a scene from the chapters in the particular lesson.
- Read that scene out loud in the group, followed by some quiet time.
- Ask group members to place themselves in the scene (as a character, or as an onlooker) so that they can imagine the emotions, responses, and thinking that may have taken place. Notice the details and the tone and imagine the interaction with the Lord that is taking place.
- Share with the group any insights that came to you in this quiet imagining.
- Allow each person in the group to thank God for some insight and to pray about some request that may have surfaced.

Sacred Reading (or Lectio Divina)

This method of prayer invites us to "listen with the ear of the heart" as St. Benedict's rule would say. We listen to the words and the phrasing, asking God to speak to our innermost being. Again, this method of prayer is most often used in an individual setting but may also be used in an adapted way within a group.

A suggested process:

- Select a scene from the chapters in the particular lesson.
- Read the scene out loud in the group, perhaps two times.
- Ask group members to ponder a word or phrase that stands out to them.
- The group members could then simply speak the word or phrase as a kind of litany of what was meaningful for your group.
- Allow time for more silence to ponder the words that were heard, asking God to reveal to you what message you are meant to hear, how God is speaking to you.
- Follow up with spoken intentions at the close of this group time.

REFLECTING ON SCRIPTURE

Reading Scripture is an opportunity not simply to learn new information but to listen to God who loves you. Pray that the same Holy Spirit who guided the formation of Scripture will inspire you to correctly understand what you read and empower you to make what you read a part of your life.

The inspired word of God contains layers of meaning. As you make your way through passages of Scripture, whether studying a book of the Bible or focusing on a biblical theme, you may find it helpful to ask yourself these four questions:

What does the Scripture passage say?
Read the passage slowly and reflectively. Become familiar with it. If the passage you are reading is a narrative, carefully observe the characters and the plot. Use your imagination to picture the scene or enter into it.

What does the Scripture passage mean?
Read the footnotes in your Bible and the commentary provided to help you understand what the sacred writers intended and what God wants to communicate by means of their words.

What does the Scripture passage mean to me?
Meditate on the passage. God's word is living and powerful. What is God saying to you? How does the Scripture passage apply to your life today?

What am I going to do about it?
Try to discover how God may be challenging you in this passage. An encounter with God contains a challenge to know God's will and follow it more closely in daily life. Ask the Holy Spirit to inspire not only your mind but your life with this living word.

CPSIA information can be obtained
at www.ICGtesting.com
Printed in the USA
BVHW091046130820
586315BV00007B/330

9 780814 665190